Fabiano Caruana expla[...]
The Ruy Lopez for club players

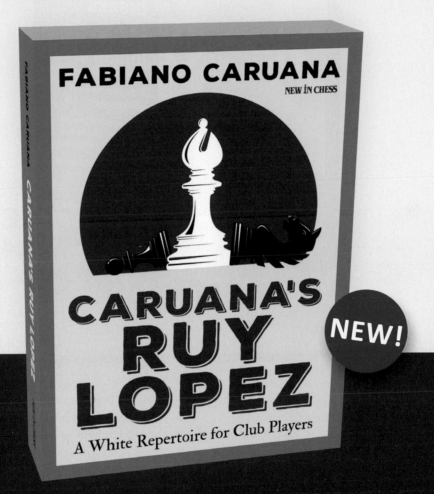

World #2 Fabiano Caruana explains his complete and practical White repertoire for club players against the Ruy Lopez, one of the most popular chess openings. It is a repertoire that every chess player will be able to understand, process, and put into practice.

This one-volume, crystal-clear repertoire covers all main variations in only 200 pages. Caruana avoids chaotic lines but doesn't shy away from sharp battles and is always looking for an advantage for White.

The book is based on Carauna's ChessBase DVD series *Navigating the Ruy Lopez*.

paperback | 208 pages | €29.95 | available at your local (chess)bookseller or at newinchess.com | a NEW IN CHESS publication

2021#6

NEW IN CHESS

6

Contents

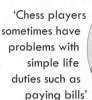

'Chess players sometimes have problems with simple life duties such as paying bills'

CONTRIBUTORS TO THIS ISSUE
Vladimir Barsky, Adhiban Baskaran, Magnus Carlsen, Jan-Krzysztof Duda, Anish Giri, Atle Grønn, Vidit Gujrathi, John Henderson, Alexandra Kosteniuk, Kamil Miton, Peter Heine Nielsen, Maxim Notkin, Judit Polgar, Matthew Sadler, Pablo Salinas, Han Schut, Sam Shankland, Jan Timman, Thomas Willemze

Zugzwang

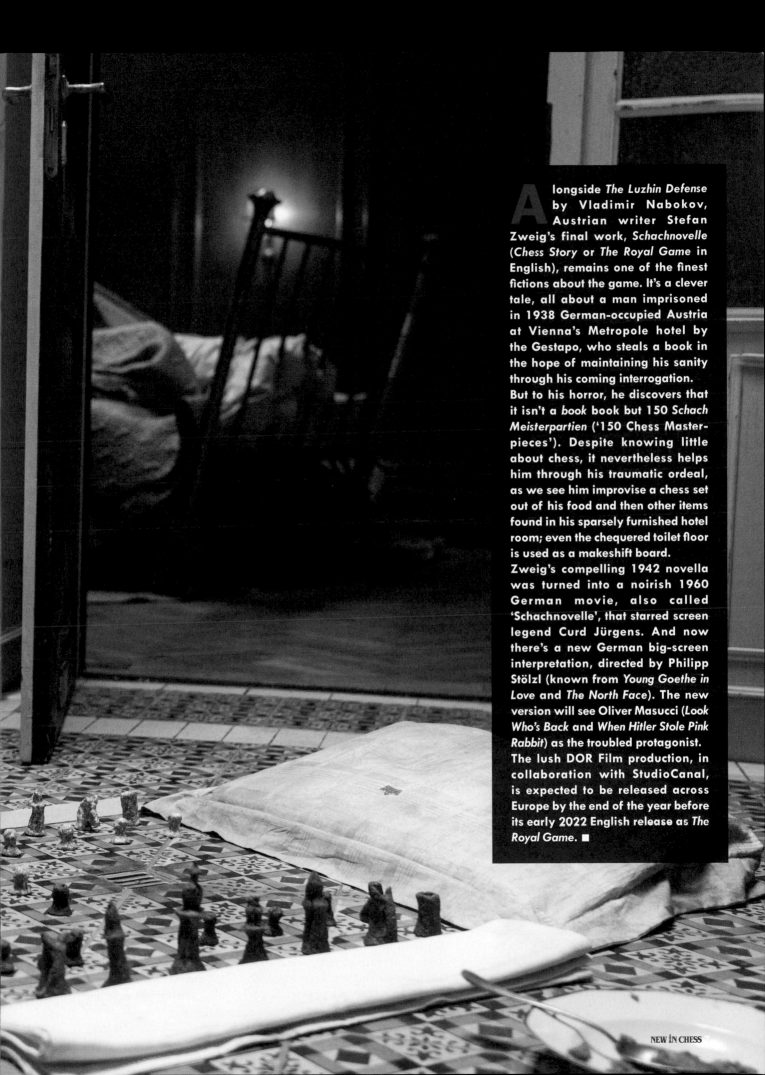

A longside *The Luzhin Defense* by Vladimir Nabokov, Austrian writer Stefan Zweig's final work, *Schachnovelle* (*Chess Story* or *The Royal Game* in English), remains one of the finest fictions about the game. It's a clever tale, all about a man imprisoned in 1938 German-occupied Austria at Vienna's Metropole hotel by the Gestapo, who steals a book in the hope of maintaining his sanity through his coming interrogation. But to his horror, he discovers that it isn't a *book* book but 150 *Schach Meisterpartien* ('150 Chess Master- pieces'). Despite knowing little about chess, it nevertheless helps him through his traumatic ordeal, as we see him improvise a chess set out of his food and then other items found in his sparsely furnished hotel room; even the chequered toilet floor is used as a makeshift board. Zweig's compelling 1942 novella was turned into a noirish 1960 German movie, also called 'Schachnovelle', that starred screen legend Curd Jürgens. And now there's a new German big-screen interpretation, directed by Philipp Stölzl (known from *Young Goethe in Love* and *The North Face*). The new version will see Oliver Masucci (*Look Who's Back* and *When Hitler Stole Pink Rabbit*) as the troubled protagonist. The lush DOR Film production, in collaboration with StudioCanal, is expected to be released across Europe by the end of the year before its early 2022 English release as *The Royal Game*. ∎

Jewel in the Crown

Isla Johnston stood out with her sublime portrayal as the younger Beth Harmon in just one episode of *The Queen's Gambit*, learning the game and developing under the

Isla 'young Beth Harmon' Johnston continues to sparkle at chess.

tutelage of her grumpy-but-lovable school caretaker Mr. Shaibel (Bill Camp). It was just one episode, but Johnston nailed the prodigy quirks and vulnerabilities for Anya Taylor-Joy to shine in the hit Netflix series.

Now the young English actress is back again at the chessboard, having been chosen by Austrian jewellery brand Swarovski to star in their new 'Welcome to Wonderlab' advertising campaign with supermodel Adwoa Aboah and *Game of Thrones*' Gwendoline Christie. The trio are all filmed grinding figures from crystals in a secret laboratory.

And keeping with her *TQG* theme, Johnston plays a futuristic steampunk version of her younger Beth in the 'Chess Room', as she becomes the brand ambassador for Swarovski's new line of crystal chess sets.

Joni's Mate

In a warm outpouring of nostalgia and admiration, music critics all over the world paid tribute to singer-songwriter Joni Mitchell on the 50th anniversary of her seminal fourth album, *Blue*. Its

release on 22 June 1971 on Reprise Records saw the Canadian being hailed overnight as an 'auteur genius'. But little did we know that we were also to discover that chess played a big part in starting the music legend off on her road to stardom.

Just as the Beatles had The Cavern in Liverpool, for Joni Mitchell it was Detroit's Chess Mate, the long forgotten venue sadly now a laundrette, where she learned her stagecraft. Back in 1963, when Morrie Widenbaum, the Michigan State Chess Champion, opened it, it was a chess club, with Bobby Fischer even playing there during his famous US Simultaneous Tour of 1964.

But chess didn't pay the bills, so Widenbaum transformed it to also accommodate the vibrant, acoustic-folk music scene of the era – and pretty soon his chess-playing coffee-house became one of Detroit's most famous and legendary blues clubs

Detroit's legendary Chess Mate, where Bobby gave a simul and Joni sang her songs.

and '60s folk clubs, attracting Bob Dylan and blues artist John Lee Hooker. Among the emerging troubadours who appeared at the venue early on their musical journeys were Gordon Lightfoot, Neil Young and Joni Mitchell.

Joni was just 21 at the time, very inexperienced, hosting intimate, dimly-lit, smoke-filled concerts with her then husband Chuck Mitchell. They entertained both separately and together and went on to log more than 60 Chess Mate performances

within 12 months, in what proved to be the incubator for her early music.

Like father, like son

The Irish Championship reached a major milestone in early August as it celebrated its centenary. The 100th edition took place in Coláiste Éanna, in Rathfarnham, Co Dublin, and was won by IM Mark Heidenfeld. Very poignantly, Heidenfeld's second national title came 40 years almost to the very day after the death of his famous father.

Mark's father, Wolfgang Heidenfeld, was a Jewish refugee born in Berlin who fled Nazi Germany for South Africa in the 1930s. There, he won the South African championship eight times. But after a chance visit to Ireland in the late 1950s, he became entranced by the Emerald Isle and moved his family there in 1961. And went on to win the Irish championship six times.

Heidenfeld senior wrote several excellent chess books, his most famous being *Draw!* (the English edition, published in 1982, of *Grosse Remispartien*, which appeared in Germany in 1968), and *Lacking the Master Touch* (1970). He died in 1981, when Mark was 13, but he bequeathed him his chess library of over 1,000 books.

Now father and son have eight Irish title wins between them. And while there have been many strong father and son players through history, the

Wolfgang's son Mark added another Irish title win to the Heidenfeld collection.

Heidenfelds are members of a very select club to have won their national championship, alongside Australia's Cecil and John Purdy with a combined six titles. If readers know of any other father/son national champions, then do please let us know.

ZugzWang

It's a busy old time for British Malaysian comedian Phil Wang, what with his first Netflix special, *Philly Philly Wang Wang*, dropping in August, and September seeing the release of his debut 'part memoir' book, *Sidesplitter: How To Be From Two Worlds At Once*. He's also

He loves chess and it's not David Howell, so this must be Phil Wang!

in the middle of a sellout UK stand-up tour that culminates in October.

And as if that isn't enough to keep anyone busy, the former introvert teen nerd, who found making people laugh to be his saving superpower, also found time in *The Guardian* to disclose that the pandemic had reconnected him with his childhood love of chess. As a result he's now addicted to playing on chess.com and following all the top chess streamers.

Wang's trigger was binge-viewing Netflix's *The Queen's Gambit*. 'I'd played a lot as a child, as you can probably tell from my face,' he self-mockingly explains. 'During a time in which nothing feels certain and life feels more open-ended than ever, I have taken refuge in chess's comforting closed system. One

board. Thirty-two pieces. Sixty-four squares. Two dorks.'

Hearing of his new-found passion for chess, resident Champions Chess Tour talking head David Howell revealed he was once mistaken for Phil Wang by a group of excited young girls while on the London Underground. 'Felt too awkward to correct them,' said the English GM on social media of his doppelgänger experience. 'So I just smiled for the selfie and said I was glad they enjoyed my stand-up show. Now I discover he's become a chess addict. The world's a funny place.'

Old in Chess

We've heard so much about preteen Grandmasters these days, but what about those achieving titles at the opposite end of the age spectrum? Like Venezuela's Salvador Diaz Carias, who in mid-June received a surprise shortly before his 88th birthday: his FIDE Master title!

FIDE acknowledged Diaz's retrospective title application based on his results in the 1960s. He won the first of his three national championship titles in 1960 and he also played for Venezuela in three Olympiads: Havana 1966 (the team's top scorer on 11½/20), Lugano 1968 (his best international performance with 10½/15) and Buenos Aires 1978.

Originally from Caracas, the sprightly octogenarian who now lives

Salvador Diaz Carias: 88 and finally an FM.

in San Cristobal is still enthralled by the game and continues to play regularly. Last year he even won a local tournament at the San Cristobal Fair.

The Porno Queen

It's amazing what you discover just by reading newspapers these days. Such as when artist Jeff Koons's ex-wife and muse Ilona Staller, better known to all as 'Cicciolina', is not performing in adult films, she turns out to be something of an avid chess player.

Ilona Staller ponders the Cicciolina Variation.

Italy's most-famous porn queen, who was once elected to the Italian parliament as a member of the Radical Party, demonstrated her chess prowess by taking part in a 'foursome' during an exhibition match in late July, as she played four players in a chess simultaneous.

Staller, 69, revealed in a lifestyle magazine that she learnt chess from her father growing up in Hungary before moving to Rome to start a film career. The match took place in a theatre in Perugia against mainly minor music and art celebs, with Staller winning two games, drawing one and losing one.

The match was staged for a good cause to help raise money for a cultural centre and museum outside Perugia. 'It's all about concentration and logic,' says Staller. 'I am not just a porno diva.' ∎

Jan-Krzysztof Duda:

'It felt natural to me that I would become World Champion one day. Now, the closer I get, the more obstacles I see.'

In the semi-final of the World Cup, a dream came to fruition as Jan-Krzysztof Duda eliminated Magnus Carlsen in a roller-coaster rapid game. Next, the Polish star stood strong again as he defeated Sergey Karjakin in the final to crown the biggest achievement of his career. The fresh Candidate talks to **DIRK JAN TEN GEUZENDAM** about his life-long love of chess, his competitiveness and the secret of his success. 'Without my mom I wouldn't have accomplished half of what I have.'

As Jan-Krzysztof Duda walked out of the customs zone on his return to Poland, he saw that the airport arrival hall was filled with family, friends and press. He was happy to see familiar faces, but was less sure about the journalists. 'We had left Sochi at 2 a.m. and I hadn't slept all night, so there was a huge chance that I'd say something stupid.' He laughs as he says it, but stresses that he finds it difficult to be the centre of attention. 'I'm an introverted person. I don't like being a star. But I want chess to become more popular in Poland and this is a golden opportunity.'

The interviews went well, perhaps because he had quickly convinced himself that the TV crews had not specifically come for him. 'That day, the Polish athletes would come back

from Tokyo, a couple of hours later, so I think they were mostly waiting for them.'

The days that followed would convincingly demonstrate that his triumph in the World Cup had really created a national outburst of enthusiasm and pride. There were more interview requests than he could handle, and countless visits to officials and sponsors – and a new sponsor. Orlen, a major Polish oil refiner and petrol retailer, offered him generous support for the next steps in his career.

In-between he met Garry Kasparov, who was guest of honour at a chess festival in Ustron, a health resort some 140 kilometres from Duda's home city of Krakow. They talked about his result in Sochi and on the forthcoming World Championship match between Carlsen and Nepomniachtchi. 'For Garry it's not that clear

that Magnus will win. I personally think that Magnus has a very good chance to win this match.'

No particular reason

A couple of days after his meeting with Kasparov, Jan-Krzysztof Duda (23) finds time for a talk on Skype. His schedule remains crammed and hectic ('I have no time at all to train chess, which kind of sucks'), but he is in an upbeat mood, talking easily and often reacting with a smile or short laugh to what he has just said.

The World Cup is a special event. You can be home in days, or you can be there for almost a month. How do you prepare for such an adventure?
'Actually, I didn't do anything special. Before the World Cup I played in Croatia and had a flight straight from there to Russia. At the start of the

'I have a very strong sense of competitiveness, in anything in life, not only in chess.'

tournament, especially during the match against Sevian, I was kind of sick. I was scared that it might be the delta variant of Covid, although I had negative PCRs and I am also vaccinated. It was not just a cold, I also had some strange symptoms. At that point, I was not thinking about qualifying for the Candidates, because I thought that to achieve that you must be healthy. I didn't put much pressure on myself and it worked. I was not feeling that well, but I was playing extremely well, at least in classical chess – mostly slow, technical games, and I avoided making a lot of mistakes. That's important in a competition in which one mistake may send you home. In the rapid games it was a bit different, but things went extremely well there too, and I see no particular reason why (laughs). It just happened, and I used my chances.'

You were very effective in the classical games, not losing a single one, and you only played four rapid games – against Grischuk and Carlsen.

'Yeah, but all of them were kind of 'psychie'. Even the first rapid game against Magnus as White. I decided to be ambitious, and got pinned terribly, and there was just one way not to lose and I managed to find it. But why put yourself in such a situation, when you can just trade pieces and make a draw? Obviously I was relying on White, like basically in all my matches in Sochi. And then I actually won my first game as Black against Magnus. That was an unexpected gift. Prior to the World Cup I had half a point out of five as Black against Magnus. Before that second rapid game I was just hoping to defend and reach the next rapid session. Somehow he

'I was not feeling that well, but I was playing extremely well'

misplayed it and then I was playing for a win, but I spoiled my advantage. I tried to be as unemotional as possible, but that is easier said than done. It was nerve-wracking and Magnus clearly didn't play his best chess, but he was under pressure for most of the game, so it wasn't all that surprising that I clinched the endgame. It just happened. It's sport. When you're under pressure, you're likely to make mistakes somewhere.'

I was following the game live and I was impressed. Even after you had lost your advantage, you kept playing with so much determination. But inside you must have been boiling...

'Yes, I was boiling, of course. The thing is I got into gambling mode. I was frustrated to have let the win slip. It looked as if Black could never lose such a position, but psychologically it was very likely that I would over-press, because I wanted to win at all cost. I also gambled when I played Bishop c3 (his 62nd move that clinched the game, see his notes on page 39 – DJtG). That was the biggest gamble in that game and actually the only winning move. Sometimes you need to be lucky.'

The wish to take risks, to take brave decisions, is what endears you to the fans. Where do you think that comes from, for an introverted person like you?

'It depends on my mood. I think I have a very strong sense of competitiveness, in anything in life, not only in chess. When I do something, I want to win, no matter what it is (laughs). That may be the reason why my chess can be so aggressive. But I see myself as a kind of universal player. I am not going all out in all my games, like Tal, for example. I like playing sharp positions, but sometimes I also feel like playing slower, more technical positions. This was the case in the World Cup, when I played very slow chess, especially as White. I think patience was one of the key factors that made me win the World Cup to. In general I am a rather impatient person, relatively speaking, of course – compared to my opponents from the chess top, let's say. But here I didn't mind playing long games, and I was very focused on what I was doing.'

Not much to lose

Many players have some kind of Magnus complex – the giant that they find it very difficult to play against. You seem to suffer less from this complex. You kept up with him at the World Blitz 2018 in Petersburg, where you finished only half a point behind him. You beat him in the Lindores rapid. You ended his undefeated streak of 125 classical games in Norway last year...

'I don't know. Magnus is an extremely strong player. He has won many games psychologically, even before the game. Actually, my first game against him, in Qatar in 2015, I lost before the game started. I don't have such a good score against Magnus,

Jan-Krzysztof Duda and his mother Wieslawa: 'She's one out of a hundred million. It's just my mom who made me such a strong player.'

because I have been really suffering as Black. But as White I have a plus score. It's difficult to say (hesitating)... For many chess fans you don't have much to lose if you play Magnus. Because you lose to the World Champion. Even if you make a draw with White it is some kind of success. That helps me in a way. There is nothing to lose and you can only win (laughs). And he's the only person in the world for whom this goes. That may be a reason, but honestly I don't know.

'Obviously, playing Magnus was not very comfortable; especially

'Patience was one of the key factors that made me win the World Cup'

in the semi-finals he was the worst person in the world to play against. I wanted to try my best, but I had negative thoughts. Sometimes my mind likes to think negatively. My overall attitude is not so optimistic. Most of the time I consider the worst possible scenarios. That I will lose two games in a row. And then I think, yes, but it's not very likely to happen; you are in good form. Such, what you might call pathetic thinking helps me to calm down, to be at ease. I don't know where it comes from. It's just me, but it's working.'

You knocked out Magnus and then you also defeated Sergey Karjakin, a former World Championship Challenger, in the final. The start was comfortable, as he got nothing from his White game.

'I think he just mixed up the move

order. Which is kind of surprising, as I had played this Vienna twice before in the World Cup. You can see Sergey was very tired if you look at his games against me. I was also tired, but I am much younger, so that was to my advantage. In the second game, I had a terrible headache, but I got such a pleasant position without risk that (starts laughing and doesn't finish his sentence)... I had been sleeping less and less, and also eating the same food for three weeks... The food in the hotel was nice, but if you eat if for two weeks you cannot stand the look of it anymore. I also ate a lot of junk food that I ordered. I was also struggling in terms of food, but I just happened to be in good form...'

Team Duda

Chess may be a solitary sport, but Jan-Krzysztof Duda is hardly left to his own devices. He often speaks about 'team Duda', and that is far from an exaggeration. At the top of the team is his mother, Wieslawa Duda, a successful businesswoman whom he calls 'my main sponsor, my manager, everything'. His mother had to raise him alone after his father suddenly died when Jan-Krzysztof was only two. Normally speaking, she would have been in Sochi, too, but other commitments forced her to stay at home and support him from a distance. At the World Cup, he was accompanied by Polish GM Kamil Miton, who has been his coach for the past ten years. And, besides his mother, he has an official manager, Adam Dzwonkowski.

Further professional advice comes from the professors, teachers and coaches of the Academy of Physical Education, where he is a student and part of a special group of athletes in various disciplines. They are coached in physical training, diets, psychology and how to deal with the media. Doing sports he finds essential for a chess player, but he has his preferences. 'Individual sports, unfortunately. Mostly swimming

and running. I go to the gym sometimes, but I think that pure strength is less useful for a chess player. I also like playing tennis and table tennis. Mostly these sports. I am not much of a football fan or football player.'

Your mother has been your companion and supporter from an early age on.
'Actually, she sensed my talent. I tried different activities when I was five, and one of them was chess. Chess was known to my family, because my aunt was Polish national women's champion in 1991, so it was not an abstract thing. My mom saw that I could focus on chess for a longer time and she signed me into the local village club. Then I met my first coach, Mr Irlik, who made me love chess. I just fell in love with chess and started to improve and improve. And I became a grandmaster at the age of 15. A lot of my games were strategic, a lot of abstract thinking. I was good at this because I studied all of Rubinstein's best games when I was very young. That gave me an advantage, compared to my rivals.

'My mom used to travel with me a lot when I was a kid, and this is probably why I avoided doing many stupid things. She spent an awful lot of her time with me. That was really cool. Without her I wouldn't have accomplished half of what I have. She's one out of a hundred million. It could not have been better for me, it's just my mom who made me such a strong player.'

A couple of times you mentioned that you had been so busy during the past few days that you didn't even have time to study chess. You are clearly missing it.
'Yes, kind of, because I have never really liked training. I very much prefer playing chess, because of my strong competitiveness. Analytical research is not really my thing, but it has to be done. A lot is studying openings with the computer. You might say that this is still

Jan-Krzysztof Duda

1998	April 26, born in Krakow, Poland
2007	U8 Polish Youth Champion
2008	U10 World Youth Champion
2012	U18 Polish Youth Champion
2012	U14 European Youth Champion
2012	International Master
2013	International Grandmaster
2014	Tromsø Olympiad, 8½/11 on Board 3 Poland
2014	European Rapid Champion
2015	Wins Lake Sevan tournament, Armenia
2015	Awarded Silver Cross of Merit by Polish President
2018	Polish Champion
2018	July, first Polish and first Junior player in world rankings
2018	Second, half a point behind Carlsen, in World Blitz Championship
2019	January, first Polish player to cross 2800 in Blitz
2020	First rapid win against Carlsen in Lindores online tournament
2020	Ends Carlsen's 125-game unbeaten streak in classical chess in Stavanger
2021	Wins World Cup and qualifies for Candidates tournament

my weakness, because studying openings is slightly different from memorizing them. I never spent much time memorizing, or training to memorize. Obviously that will change. It's great to compare me and my rival in Poland, Radoslaw Wojtaszek. We are exact opposites in terms of training and attitude towards chess. He prepares, like, three weeks before a tournament, a couple of hours each day memorizing variations, all the variations that could be useful. I sometimes memorize before the game, maybe a couple of hours, and it's often hit or miss, and I have blackouts. Actually, I am capable of digesting a lot of material in a short time, but sometimes it's just too much. And it's tricky to play against guys like Magnus Carlsen, who can basically play anything. You just have to guess. And I actually managed to guess his Bishop b5 check in the second rapid game.

'Besides openings, I study endgames, play training games, analyse my games. And I possibly like playing online chess too much (laughs), of which maybe 10 percent is useful. But it's just my favourite way to spend my free time – better than watching TV or whatever. Blitz, bullet, with increments, but 1-0 is also okay. These faster time-controls are tricky if you play Firouzja or one of these younger guys. But of course it's just for fun. It has nothing to do with real chess.'

Only chess or also other games?
'No, mostly chess, 99.9 per cent (laughs).'

Chess books in 15 languages

For a player of your age you have a remarkable chess library. Where did that love for books come from?
'When I started chess back in 2005, there obviously were some Fritzes and other programs, and I used them, but I have always liked studying chess from books as well. It's been very natural for me from a very young age. And I've been collecting them. A couple of thousand books, and also magazines. Many were gifts from older players, and there are a lot of Soviet books. And I like buying books in foreign countries. I've got a Chinese book, one in Hebrew (laughs). It's not that I read them, but I have chess books in 15 languages.'

Which books would you recommend, books that had a special impact on you?
'I can recommend Kasparov's *My Great Predecessors*, of course. I grew up on those books. A nice combination of analysis and stories. I spent really a lot of time studying them, even to this day I still look at them. It

'Playing online chess is my favourite way to spend my free time. But it's just for fun. It has nothing to do with real chess.'

also depends on what level of players we are talking about. For instance, Gelfand's books... they are very good, but they are really tough. There are many good books. I also like biographies, games collections of the best players in the world.

'But I also like to read about openings. I like to get the New In Chess Yearbooks. Especially the Yearbooks, because it's always like a rush of adrenaline. You get the condensed knowledge of openings from the last months. It's always a special moment when you get a package and you realize it probably contains a Yearbook. Very nice. I usually acquaint myself with all the material in a couple of hours, and then it's no longer that rush of adrenaline, but nice emotions.'

And you are interested the history of the game...
'Yeah, yeah, I was crazy about that actually. When I was eight years old, I read about all the World Champions, starting from Steinitz. When they won their matches for the World Championship and when they lost their title. I was really into it, one could say. I had that chess culture, and I also knew their best games, and that was very profitable for me at that age.'

You were a great talent and became a grandmaster at a young age. What is the feeling now in Poland? That you are fulfilling a dream that has been in the making for so many years?
'Yeah, (with a laugh) I think I was crazy actually, when I was seven

or eight years old. I was a workaholic, working on chess six hours a day. I got a gift from my first trainer, this big Polgar tactics book of five thousand positions. I was solving these tactics because I wanted to. I can't see this happening today. For me, doing tactics is my least favourite thing to do. I really have to force myself. Of course it's an important thing, to grasp patterns and use your brain. But back then I was doing it out of free will, I was definitely kind of crazy.

'As said, competitiveness was key for me. I quickly became good at chess and dominated my age groups. Then I started playing against older guys and winning games. I became World Champion U10 in Vung Tau, in Vietnam, in 2008. That was of course a milestone. It was very natural for me to study chess, to play chess, and it is to this day. I can't really imagine myself not playing chess. If chess didn't exist in the real world, it would be difficult to come up with some other activity. It's been so natural for me, since early childhood. 'It was also very natural to me that I would become the World Champion one day. When I was six, seven years old, that was obvious to me. Now, the closer I get, the more obstacles I see on the way, I am not so sure about it anymore (laughs).'

First, there is going to be the Candidates tournament, and then possibly a match. What will be the plan?
'I will have to add more players to my team and prepare, because this is going to be something entirely different. Maybe the Candidates will be in the second part of 2022. If, say, the Candidates were to take place a week from now, it would be better for me, as I am an intuitive player. I like such challenges, whereas other players must be thoroughly prepared. But that's not the case, so there will be a lot of tough preparation. It will be done, but I am not really looking forward to it.' ∎

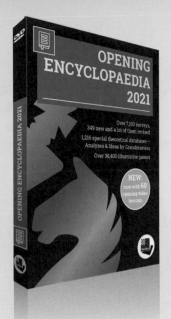

OPENING ENCYCLOPAEDIA 2021

The comprehensive theoretical reference work for beginners and pros alike

The new Opening Encyclopaedia 2021 is a collection of all the opening articles from all the issues of ChessBase Magazine and covers with more than 1,200 articles the whole gamut of openings. An enormous treasure trove of ideas and high-level analysis! In the new edition, as usual the number of articles has increased – compared to the previous year 66 new opening articles as well as 349 new opening surveys have been added. The menu structure offers comfortable access to all tutorials and articles. Under the main categories "Open games", "Semi-open games", "Closed openings", "Semi closed openings", "English Opening and Reti" and "Flank openings" you will find all the recommendations and analyses classified according to the names of the openings.

Compared to the previous edition the number of opening videos has been increased by another 50 %! 60 selected videos with the most popular Chess-Base authors – e.g. Daniel King, Simon Williams, Yannick Pelletier, Jan Werle, Mihail Marin, Erwin l'Ami – await you. That represents a total of over 22 hours of the best chess entertainment!

The connection between the opening tutorials and the special opening articles has also been improved: the tutorials are introductory texts on all known areas both for familiarisation for beginners as well an orientation for advanced players. Each opening is presented in the tutorials in brief. In the new addition, the tutorials now offer links to the advanced and in-depth opening articles that are available in the Opening Encyclopaedia 2021.

How can you improve your repertoire with new ideas and tricky lines? Or do you want to try something completely different? Let yourself be inspired and see which opening suits you best!

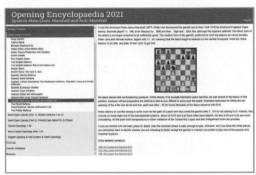

All innovations at a glance:

- Over 1,200 opening articles with professional analyses by prestigious title holders
- 60 opening videos by the most popular ChessBase authors – total running time: over 22 hours
- 7,127 opening surveys, 349 new, created by GM Lubomir Ftacnik
- Database with all 39,200 games from the opening articles
- Intuitive menu structure, classification by opening name, rapid and easy access

Opening Encyclopaedia 2021   99.90 €

Update from
Opening Encyclopaedia 2020   69.90 €

ChessBase GmbH · News: en.chessbase.com · CB Shop: shop.chessbase.com
CHESSBASE DEALER: NEW IN CHESS · P.O. Box 1093 · NL-1810 KB Alkmaar
phone (+31)72 5127137 · fax (+31)72 5158234 · WWW.NEWINCHESS.COM

Duda shines in Sochi World Cup

A view of the playing hall at the start of the first round. On the left, Pablo Salinas is still unaware that he is going to create a masterpiece against Mads Andersen.

After three long weeks of 'in person' chess, Jan-Krzysztof Duda stole the limelight from Magnus Carlsen as he emerged victorious at the 2021 World Cup. With his win, 'JKD' qualified for the next Candidates tournament, as did runner-up Sergey Karjakin. **VLADIMIR BARSKY** watched hundreds of delighted chess players meet again, and introduces the highlights of a great FIDE event.

In the vast exhibition hall of the 2018 Chess Olympiad in Batumi, the stand of the Belarussian Chess Federation was bustling with activity. Delegates were treated to snacks and drinks and urged to vote for Minsk as the venue for the 2021 World Cup and the 2022 Olympiad. The hospitality paid off, and the FIDE Congress honoured the bid of the Belarus capital. A few months later, FIDE president Arkady Dvorkovich made a special trip to Minsk to meet with President Alexander Lukashenko, who confirmed all these agreements.

However, both events were left

hanging in the air when in the spring of 2020, a few months before the start of mass protests in Belarus, the country's leadership reneged on its obligations without giving any reason. Dvorkovich declared that FIDE would demand monetary compensation from Belarus, 'which did not act like a partner', but it is hard to believe that any money will be forthcoming. What did happen, is that Russia came to the rescue, or more precisely the mountain resort Krasnaya Polyana, which is part of the city of Sochi. The 2015 Women's World Championship had already been held here, and the place is great for chess battles: fresh air, quiet and calm – there are no crowds of tourists like in Sochi on the coast. True, the weather during the tournament was rather hot, but the players were provided with transfers to the tournament hall and back.

Despite the pandemic and in the face of many logistic challenges, FIDE decided to expand the number of participants, so that as many players from as many different countries as possible could test their strength against the strongest, or at least just play in the same hall with Magnus Carlsen, Fabiano Caruana, Levon Aronian, Alexander Grischuk and other giants. Over 300 chess players from almost 100 countries gathered in Krasnaya Polyana. In these days of Covid, it took some players several days to travel, but no one complained – as everyone had missed playing 'live' chess so much.

For one reason or another, 17 prominent names declined to participate, including the winner and runner-up of last World Cup, Teimour Radjabov and Ding Liren, Women's World Champion Ju Wenjun and former champion Vishy Anand, as well as the strongest Russian GM Ian Nepomniachtchi, who preferred to focus on his preparation for the World Championship match.

The organizers took strict measures to combat Covid: spectators were not allowed into the playing hall, and not only all players, but also referees, accredited journalists, staff of the organizing committee and all service personnel underwent PCR tests every three days. The arbiters urged the players not to shake hands, and many wore masks, although the rules did not require this. But once the number of participants had sharply decreased, people started shaking hands again, and almost all players stopped wearing masks in the hall.

Dazzling brilliancy

In the first round, 156 participants took part. Each round consisted of mini-matches of two games with classical time-control. If the score was 1-1, there was a tie-break in the form of additional rapid games and, if necessary, an Armageddon blitz game. In the second round, the winners of the first stage were joined by 50 seeded grandmasters led by World Champion Magnus Carlsen.

With so many games being played, it is impossible to give a full account of the World Cup. Out of necessity, we will limit ourselves to a selection of highlights that not only show some

It took some players several days to travel, but no one complained – as everyone had missed playing 'live' chess so much

of the best and most exciting chess that was played in Sochi, but that are also key moments in the knockout race as it unfolded.

The most sensational game of the first round was played by Pablo Salinas. In a brilliant attack with dazzling sacrifices reminiscent of the 19th century, the Chilean grandmaster stunned Danish GM Mads Andersen. Salinas was knocked out in the second round by Peter Svidler, but this brilliancy will forever be linked to his name.

From the venue the players had a stunning view of the mountains around Krasnaya Polyana.

NOTES BY
Pablo Salinas

Mads Andersen
Pablo Salinas
Sochi World Cup 2021 (1.1)
Slav Defence, Semi-Slav

Before arriving in Sochi, I played two tournaments in Philadelphia since, like many players, I had not played in person for over a year! Although my performances in the US were nothing special, they helped me acclimatize and play with confidence in the World Cup.

1.♘f3 d5 2.e3
A surprise. According to my database, Mads Andersen plays 2.g3 every time he opens with ♘f3.
2...♘f6 3.c4 c6 4.♘c3 e6 5.b3 ♗d6 6.d4

Transposing to a Semi-Slav, in which I felt comfortable and confident about my position.
6...0-0 7.♕c2 ♘bd7 8.♗e2 b6 9.0-0 ♗b7 10.♗b2 ♕e7 11.♖ad1 ♖ad8 12.♖fe1 ♖fe8 13.♗f1
We had both played fairly quickly so far.
13...c5 14.cxd5 exd5 15.g3 ♖c8

Luckily, this position was familiar, since I had played it a week earlier at the World Open in Philadelphia.
16.♗h3
On that occasion the game continued 16.♕b1 c4 17.bxc4 ♗b4 18.♘d2 dxc4 19.♗h3 ♗xc3 20.♗xc3 ♘e4 21.♘xe4 ♗xe4, with a nice blocking position for Black (0-1, 60, Sinha-Salinas, Philadelphia World Open 2021).
16...cxd4
Earlier this year, 16...c4 17.bxc4 ♖xc4 18.♘d2 ♖c7 was played, with a draw after 42 moves in Esipenko-Giri, Wijk aan Zee 2021.
17.♘xd4
17.exd4 ♘e4 leads to an interesting and complex position without the classical isolated queen's pawn.
17...♗b4
Continuing to put pressure on c3.

18.♘de2?
The only move was 18.f3, in order to avoid the continuations with ...♘e4. To meet this, I had planned 18...a6, with an interesting position for both sides, in which White plays against the isolated pawn and Black tries to exploit the weakness on e3.
18...♘e4?
A natural move that tries to increase the pressure on c3 but that misses an important detail...
The correct move was 18...♘e5! 19.♗g2 (19.♗xc8 loses to 19...♘f3+ 20.♔g2 ♖xc8 21.♔xf3 d4+ 22.e4 ♘xe4) 19...d4! (exploiting the opening of the long diagonal) 20.♖xd4 ♗c5 21.♖dd1 ♗xg2 22.♔xg2 ♕b7+ 23.e4 ♗xf2, and the threats of ...♘eg4 and ...♘fg4 are very strong. Black is winning.

19.a3??
The strong and only move was 19.♕xe4!!. Both Mads and I had seen this move, but for some reason we both concluded that Black would be better, missing a fairly simple continuation: 19...dxe4 20.♖xd7 ♕e5 21.♖xb7 ♗xc3 22.♗xc3 ♖xc3 23.♘xc3 ♕xc3 24.♖d1!.

According to the engine, this position is equal, but I think it is Black who should be careful in view of the threats on the seventh row after moves like ♖xa7, ♖dd7 and ♗f1, seeking to pressurize the f7-pawn. Perhaps the story would have been different...
19...♘xf2!
The idea behind ...♘e4. Black is winning.

20.axb4

White can't take the knight: 20.♔xf2 ♛xe3+ 21.♔f1 (or 21.♔g2 d4+ 22.♔f1 ♛f3+ 23.♔g1 ♛h1+ 24.♔f2 ♛xh2+ 25.♗g2 ♛xg2 mate) 21...♛f3+ 22.♔g1 ♗c5+ 23.♘d4 ♗xd4+ 24.♖xd4 ♖xe1+ 25.♗f1 ♖xf1 mate.

In case of 20.♗xd7 Black has the winning 20...♘xd1, with the threat of ...♛xe3+.

20...♘xh3+

21.♔f1

21.♔g2 loses to 21...d4+ 22.♔xh3 ♛e6+ 23.g4 ♛h6+ 24.♔g3 ♖xe3+ 25.♔f2 ♛xh2+ 26.♔f1 ♖f3, mate.

21...♛xe3

Here I thought the game was over.

22.♛f5

Suddenly I started worrying... My first option was to play ...d4, and although it's a good move, I did not see a completely clear continuation. Then I evaluated 22...♛e6, but despite Black's material advantage it was not decisive. After thinking for several minutes I found a nice continuation:

22...♘f6! After 22...♛e6? 23.♘d4 ♛xf5+ 24.♘xf5 ♖xe1+ 25.♖xe1, despite being down two pawns,

Pablo Salinas: 'The number of messages that I got made me realize how special the game was. So much so that even the Russian media talked about it!'

White has compensation due to the activity of his pieces.

23.♗c1

The knight on h3 is untouchable, e.g. 23.♛xh3 ♛f3+ 24.♔g1 ♘g4 25.♛g2 (or 25.♖f1 ♛e3+ 26.♔h1 d4+, and Black wins) 25...♛e3+ 26.♔f1 d4, with a multitude of threats.

23...♘g4!

The idea behind 22...♘f6 – the queen cannot be captured.

24.♖d3 24.♗xe3 ♘xe3 is not only a fork; it's also mate!

24...d4! 25.♖ed1 Again the queen could not be taken because of the threat of mate, now with ...♘xh2.

25...♛g1+

The third and final queen sacrifice. Now the capture is unavoidable.

26.♘xg1 ♘xh2 Mate.

Thanks to Mads for the sporting gesture of allowing the game to end with checkmate. It is something that doesn't happen very often.

As for me, the truth is that I was very happy to have won, since it meant that I was one step closer to the next round. But when I got to the hotel, the number of messages I received about the game made me realize how special it was. So much so that even the Russian national media talked about it!

Leaving Sochi

Every round, half of the participants vanished, but it wasn't only the chess that was making victims. The unpleasant news of the second round was that Levon Aronian, two-time World Cup winner, had to leave Sochi due to illness. His PCR test was ambiguous, but the symptoms were not good, and Aronian decided not to risk either his own health or that of those around him. Next, the Indonesian player Susanto Megaranto turned out to be positive. He was forced to withdraw after 15 moves in his game with Fabiano Caruana. Unfortunately, the medical laboratory did not have time to check all the tests before the start of the round, so their game had to be interrupted. Together with Megaranto, two compatriots with whom he had made the long journey to Sochi had to leave. None of the Indonesian players got sick, but a representative of their delegation was hospitalized in Krasnodar with a severe form of Covid – fortunately he had recovered by the end of the tournament.

Fabiano Caruana did not get infected, but his elimination at the hands of Kazakh grandmaster Rinat Jumabaev was the biggest sensation of the third round. Perhaps the vice-World Champion failed to warm up in Sochi. In the first round, he rested because of his high rating, and in the second his opponent had to leave. And the surprises of Round 3 did not end with Caruana's departure, as two more favourites were knocked out: Anish Giri and Shakhriyar Mamedyarov.

Among the players who were doing very well was Sam Shankland. In our previous issue, the American expressed his self-confidence after his fine victory in Prague, and in Sochi he was equally determined on the board. In Round 5, Shankland got the better of World Cup legend Peter Svidler. The way Shankland was knocked out in the next round by Sergey Karjakin rightfully left him filled with regret and self-reproach, but this was a win that he will cherish.

NOTES BY
Sam Shankland

Sam Shankland
Peter Svidler
Sochi World Cup 2021 (5.2)
King's Indian Defence, Sämisch Variation

While Rounds 2-4 were hardly stress-free, I did manage to get through them in one piece and advance to the Sweet 16 without being the unfortunate victim of an early upset. But in the Sweet 16, I found myself facing Peter Svidler, a legend of the previous generation, and one of the best World Cup performers of all time. I knew there would be a tough match in store for me, and I was very happy to defeat a strong player to advance to the quarter final.

1.d4 ♘f6 2.c4 g6 3.h4!?

I had not been particularly worried about my black game against Peter, which had ended in a draw the previous day. I told my team that I would be fine on my own and that I was confident that I could equalize and get a playable position. And I told them to just focus completely on the Grünfeld for two days and to have their best idea ready for me. When they told me I would be playing 3.h4, I was rather surprised! I had never even checked it before and did not have any file on it in my opening-master base. I was sceptical of doing something so hyper-modern, but ultimately I am glad that I kept an open mind.

3...♗g7 4.♘c3 d6
While 3.h4 is the ultimate anti-Grün-

feld, preventing ...d7-d5, it looks a bit out of place against a King's Indian. The point of h2-h4 is most clear if Black insists upon playing a Grünfeld at all cost with 4...d5. After 5.h5! ♘xh5 6.cxd5 e6 7.g4! ♘f6 8.dxe6 ♗xe6 9.e4! Black has a very dangerous position, as was seen in a recent encounter between Vachier-Lagrave and Nepomniachtchi.

4...♘c6 is an interesting move order for Black as well, and the one Peter recommended in his recently published Grünfeld course on Chessable. He did quite a good job overall, but somewhere within the analysis of 4...♘c6 I found something I think he had missed. Let's leave it at that.

5.e4 ♘c6

6.♘ge2! Just a week after this game, Fedoseev tried 6.d5 instead against Carlsen, and got clobbered. I think ♘ge2 is a better move. After 6...♘e5! the knight on e5 is much more secure than it normally is in a structure like this, because f2-f4 can always be met by ...♘eg4. The knight then will remain on an excellent square without fear of being kicked with h2-h3. Magnus went on to win a brilliant game.

6...0-0 7.f3

I was sceptical of doing something so hyper-modern as 3.h4!?, but I am glad that I kept an open mind

We have now transposed to an unusual Sämisch King's Indian. Peter played a well-known motif in the style of a young Garry Kasparov's famous game against Lputian:

7...e5! 8.d5 ♘d4! This is formally a novelty, but any novelty that the computer gives as its best move can hardly be considered a novelty at all. I had checked it before the game.

9.♗e3 c5 10.dxc6 bxc6 11.♘xd4 exd4 12.♗xd4

12...♖b8

Peter played this move very fast, suggesting he was still in his preparation, but I suspect he may have confused himself on the move order. According to my analysis, it was better to play ...c6-c5 first and only then play ...♖b8, depending on where White moves his bishop.

I believe 12...c5! is the best move. Black will clearly have to play it sooner or later, and it turns out that he should play the position very differently depending on where White puts his bishop.

– 13.♗f2, then, is White's most consistent move, with the plan I executed in the game, but now Black does not need to play ...♖b8. After 13...♘h5! 14.♕c2 f5! he is getting counterplay from another angle, and he looks fine to me.

– After 13.♗e3, 13...♖b8! makes sense, because my ♕c2 plan will not work: 14.♕c2? (14.♕d2 should have be preferred, but I still think

after 14...♘h5 15.0-0-0 ♕a5 Black has good counterplay. This is exactly the kind of position in which White wants his bishop on f2 in order to be able to come back to e1 and support the c3-knight) 14...♘h5! 15.0-0-0 ♘g3!, and Black gets too much counterplay. The bishop was needed on f2.

13.♕c2!

This move looks a bit unnatural, but I like it. Putting the queen on c2 rather than d2 allows the bishop to regroup to e1 very nicely, and it is easier for White to take on d6 with the rook than it is with the bishop.

13...c5 14.♗f2 ♗e6

It was not too late to play for ...f7-f5 with 14...♘h5. This chance has now come and gone. After 15.0-0-0 the c5-pawn is hanging, and Black must play 15...♕a5 (not 15...f5? 16.♗xc5!, White winning), but after 16.♗e1 White looks better to me.

15.0-0-0

15...♘d7!

Peter correctly surmised that energetic play was called for. Black's position is strategically suspect – after all, he is a pawn down. So he must look for direct counterplay and should not worry about losing a second pawn. This was the first time I took a real think during the game. I knew White was better from my preparation, but I also understood that the position was so dynamic and complicated that one mistake could easily spell disaster, and that the objective evaluation would matter a lot less than how well I handled the resulting chaos. This is the start of every King's Indian story! What I came up with was not the best, but certainly interesting.

16.♖xd6 When I played this move, I understood that I would lose the c4-pawn. My goal was to get f3-f4 and e4-e5 in, blunting the g7-bishop, but things were not as easy as I would have liked them to be.

16.f4! was the best move, its main point being that it prevents the manoeuvre ...♘d7-e5-c6, and I think Black's knight will end up an ineffective attacker. After 16...♕a5 17.♗e1 ♘b6 18.b3 White is clearly better.

16...♕a5 17.♗e1 ♘e5

18.f4?!
Still following my plan.
18.h5! was the best move. I was worried about 18...♗xc4 19.f4 ♗xf1, but the machine is totally unfazed by White's ridiculous structure. After 20.fxe5 ♗c4 21.hxg6 fxg6 22.♘a4! ♕b5 23.b3! Black is facing very real problems. The e-pawn is coming.

18...♘xc4 19.♗xc4 ♗xc4 20.e5

When I took my long think on move 16, I had calculated this far, realized that Black couldn't take a2, and was satisfied with my position thanks to my extra pawn, the blunted g7-bishop, and h4-h5 on the way. But I had seriously underestimated Black's next move.

20...♖fd8!
Simply developing and challenging my rook on d6. I knew I did not want to let him capture it to open up the g7-bishop, but if I traded rooks on d8, it would make it much easier for Black to take on a2 in the future.
After 20...♗xa2? 21.♘d5! Black's queen is nearly trapped, and after 21...♕b5 22.♘e7+! ♔h8 23.h5! White should deliver mate in short order.
20...h5 was a move that concerned me for a moment, as Black has prevented h4-h5. But White can play in the style of the Dragon and start throwing stuff with 21.g4!, and I suspect Black will get mated.

21.♖xd8+ ♖xd8 22.h5

22...♗xa2!
Now Black can safely grab this pawn. I will not be able to give checkmate

with ♘c3-d5-e7, because Black's king can hide on f8, thanks in no small part to his excellent decision to play ...♖f8-d8.

23.hxg6 hxg6?!
This move is not bad objectively, but it feels very dangerous to me. Black's king is really inviting trouble.
I was expecting 23...fxg6. After 24.♘xa2 ♕xa2 25.♗c3 I thought White should be a bit better thanks to the pawn structure and the bad bishop on g7. But the machine disagrees and insists on absolute equality.

24.♘e4
When I played this, I was nearly certain that 24...♕b5 was the only move. It turns out that 24...♕a6 also holds, but I started getting hopeful when Peter did not respond right away, and indeed he ended up missing an important detail.

24...♕b6?
In a position this sharp, one oversight is immediately decisive.
24...♕b5! should have been preferred, keeping the queen on a safer square. I thought White was better after 25.♘d6, but the machine claims Black is fine. Still, I understood this was his best option, even if my evaluation was overly optimistic.
As said, the weird 24...♕a6 also holds. I thought Black could resign after 25.♗h4, because the c5-pawn is hanging, but the computer claims that even after the seriously depressing response 25...♖c8! Black is quite okay.

25.♗h4!
I took a few minutes to double-check

that I had not missed anything, but indeed I had not, and White wins.

25...♖d4

26.♘f6+!

At first I thought 26.♗e7? might win too, but I then noticed Black could save the day with 26...♗b3!.

26...♚f8 27.♗f2!

A silent retreating move spells Black's fate. He is unable to bring the rook to c4 because of the fork on d7. But what else can he do? The rook is hit, and it cannot move without a mate on c5.

27...♗xf6

At this point, I knew White was winning with ♗xd4, but somehow it looked a bit annoying to break down Black's position after a subsequent ...♗e7 and ...♗e6. I realized that if I could find a way to take on f6, this would simplify my task considerably, and while I had a blind spot for a while, I eventually found the way. After 27...♖c4 28.♕xc4 ♗xc4, 29.♗xc5+ is the most precise: after 29...♕xc5 30.♘d7+ it is time to resign.

28.exf6!

After 28.♗xd4 ♗e7 29.♗c3 ♗e6 White is surely winning, but it didn't seem that easy to me somehow. The

Sam Shankland was happy to qualify for the FIDE Grand Prix, but the way the American was knocked out in the quarter-finals will haunt him for a long time to come.

queen is coming to a6 next, there are no immediate threats, and my pieces don't coordinate too well. I think 28.exf6 was a much simpler solution.

28...♕xf6 29.♕xc5+ ♖d6 30.♕c8+

For whatever reason, after 30...♚e7, I had a blind spot in my calculation and missed the simple 31.♗h4 for a

long time, instead looking at moves like ♕c7, ♖e1, ♗c5, etc. But once I noticed it, there was nothing else to be done.

Peter resigned here, as 30...♚g7 would allow a mate on h8, while 30...♖d8 would allow 31.♕xd8+, 32.♖h8+, and 33.♗h4+.

I was very happy with myself for beating such a strong and accomplished player, and in regulation, to make it through to the quarter final and qualify for the FIDE Grand Prix. I lost a heart-breaking quarter final to Karjakin, in which I beat him in the first game, and in the first playoff game as well, only to lose Games 2 and 4 to let him back into the match. While that one will haunt me for a long time, I was quite satisfied with what I produced in the Sweet 16.

I was very happy with myself for beating such a strong and accomplished player, and to make it through to the quarter final and qualify for the FIDE Grand Prix

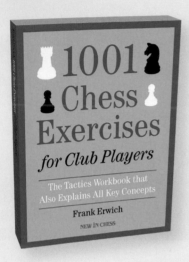
Last of the Indians

India has rapidly become a chess superpower, with the number of GMs growing almost weekly. The last remaining Indian in the World Cup in Round 5 was Vidit Gujrathi, currently the country's second player after Vishy Anand. Vidit clearly meant business and played good, strong chess. With the following win he earned a spot in the quarter finals.

NOTES BY
Vidit Gujrathi

Vasif Durarbayli
Vidit Gujrathi
Sochi World Cup 2021 (5.2)
Ruy Lopez, Arkhangelsk Variation

This was the first time in my World Cup experience that I had gone beyond Round 3. All my matches so far had been quite hard-fought, and this one was no exception. In the first game, after I missed a winning chance, I was lost for the most part but Durarbayli was unable to finish me off.

1.e4 e5 2.♘f3 ♘c6 3.♗b5 a6 4.♗a4 ♘f6 5.0-0 b5 6.♗b3 ♗c5

I hadn't played the Arkhangelsk before, but that didn't seem to surprise my opponent too much. He blitzed out his next moves, anyways.

7.a4 ♖b8 8.♘xe5 ♘xe5 9.d4 ♗xd4 10.♕xd4 d6 11.♗f4 c5 12.♕e3 c4 13.♗a2

13...♘h5!?
An interesting new and direct approach to target the dark-squared bishop. Also, a move which made my opponent finally stop and think.
Levon Aronian, Anish Giri and Fabiano Caruana had all played 13...0-0, but I didn't fancy the positions after 14.♘c3 b4 15.♘e2, with a white edge.
14.♘c3 Trying to avoid the exchange with 14.♗g5 f6 15.♗h4 g5 won't help the bishop.
14...♘xf4 15.♕xf4 0-0 16.axb5 axb5 17.♖ad1 ♗e6
A slight inaccuracy. Starting with 17...b4 would have avoided some options.

18.♗b1 18.b4, followed by ♘e2, c3, ♗b1-c2, would finally enable the bishop to break from its cage.
18...b4 19.♘e2
The position felt fairly equal. So far, I had played all my moves fast. I realized that if White managed to play c2-c3 and free the bishop, he would be quite comfortable.
19...♕b6! A very tricky move, which I feel made me win the game! Vasif Durarbayli thought that ...♗g4 was the only threat in the position. But I had a cunning idea up my sleeve.

Vidit Gujrathi and Vasif Durarbayli show how tense chess can be.
It's the bishop on b1 – a mere pawn! – that will do White in.

An important decision. Initially, I was trying all the queen moves to protect c3 and then bring the knight to d2. But all lines give White some counterplay. For instance: 25...♕b4 26.♔h2! ♘c4 27.♖d4!, and the pin is really annoying. And 25...♕b2 26.♖xd6 ♘c4 27.♖c6 ♘d2 28.♕xc3 ♕xc3 29.♖xc3 ♖fb8 would win a piece, but it's not so clear.

26.♔h2 In order to play f4.

26...♖a3

Defending the pawn in order to play ...♘c4-d2. Surprisingly, White had an unexpected defensive idea here. Therefore, 26...♕b4 with the same idea of ...♘c4, would have been more effective.

27.♖e3?!

Missing the only chance in the game. After 27.f4 ♘c4 the immediate 28.f5 f6 doesn't lead to much.

But White had 28.♖d3!!, and now:

ANALYSIS DIAGRAM

– After 28...♘d2 it looks as if the bishop on b1 is lost, but White gets unexpected counterplay on the kingside: 29.f5! ♕b8! (keeping an eye on the king. 29...f6 runs into 30.e5!!, followed by either ♖d7 or f6) 30.f6 g6

20.h3?! 20.♕d2! was the only way to avoid the trick in the game.

20...c3! 21.bxc3 Here 21.b3 is a type of move that is extremely difficult to make! Just look at the bishop on b1 ☺. **21...♗c4! 22.♖fe1 ♗xe2 23.♖xe2 bxc3**

Now we see the point of 19...♕b6. I could have reached the same position without h3 and ...♕b6 included, but then White could have played ♗a2 and freed the bishop.

24.♖ee1

24.♗a2 loses a piece to 24...♕a6!.

24...♖a8 It's important to keep the b1-bishop boxed in! Now, if I manage to get my knight to c4/d2, it would just be winning, although it's not easy, as my c3-pawn is constantly under pressure.

24...♕a6 was another way to keep the bishop locked up. In some lines, the queen ends up on a1, which seemed a little odd to me.

25.♕g3

25...♖fc8!

My coach Alon Greenfeld texted: 'Congrats, Vidit with the win. In my long career, I have never seen a pawn on the 1st rank!'

31.♕g5! ♔h8 32.♕d5! ♖f8 33.♗a2! and finally, with a series of accurate moves, the white bishop gets a second life ☺ and the chances are equal.
– After 28...♖a1 White has an unexpected resource as well. Chess is full of amazing ideas, sadly enough, they are usually left behind the scenes, because humans can't play like Stockfish yet! 29.♖xc3 ♖xb1 30.♕g4!! (Black has back rank problems!) 30...♖c5 31.♖xb1 ♕xb1 32.♖b3 h5! 33.♕d7 ♕f1 34.♖b8+ ♔h7 35.♕xf7 ♘e3 36.♕g8+ ♔g6 37.♕e8+ ♔h7 leads to a crazy draw.

27...♕b4!

Now everything is secure. There is no way for White to stop the idea of ...♘c4-d2.

28.f4 ♘c4 29.♕g4 ♖b8 30.♖g3 g6 31.f5

The attack on the kingside looks dangerous, but it's harmless. The key

for Black is not to hurry in capturing the bishop on b1; it's dead anyways. Once he brings back his queen in the defence, White is doomed.

31...♘d2 32.♕f4 ♕d4!

Making it abundantly clear that Black is winning.

33.fxg6

Or 33.f6 ♕e5, and Black wins.

33...hxg6 34.♖g5 ♖a1 35.♖d5 ♕xe4 36.♕xd6

36...♖axb1!

Finally the poor soul is captured!

37.♖d4 ♕e6 38.♕c7 ♕b6

My opponent resigned and I was through to the quarter finals!
I received many nice messages after the game, but the message of my coach Alon Greenfeld stood out: 'Congrats, Vidit with the win. In my long career, I have never seen a pawn on the 1st rank!' That aptly summarizes the game! ☺

Slowly but surely

In the meantime, Magnus Carlsen was doing what was expected from him, but the World Champion was not sweeping the field. In Round 4, he only shook off Radek Wojtaszek in the rapid tie-break, and in his next match, a tense tussle with Russian youngster Andrey Esipenko, he only prevailed in the blitz games. Carlsen took the next hurdle, Etienne Bacrot of France, in the quarter finals with remarkable ease. Having won the first game, the top-seed even declined his opponent's draw offer in the second game and went on to win 2-0.

One of the other winners in the quarter finals was Jan-Krzysztof Duda. The Polish grandmaster had slowly but surely made his way through the rounds without big frights. Soon his name would be on everyone's lips. But first he put an end to the hopes of Vidit Gujrathi.

NOTES BY
Anish Giri

Jan-Krzysztof Duda
Vidit Gujrathi
Sochi World Cup 2021 (6.2)
Ruy Lopez, Arkhangelsk Variation

1.e4

Jan-Krzysztof Duda is not known for going down long forcing lines, but in this game this was exactly what happened.

1...e5 2.♘f3 ♘c6 3.♗b5 a6 4.♗a4 ♘f6 5.0-0 b5 6.♗b3 ♗c5

Vidit had previously shown a few of his weapons against 1.e4, the Arkhangelsk Variation being the latest and most successful one, as he beat Vasif Durarbayli with it in the previous round. This choice obviously would no longer be a surprise, and JKD goes on to blitz out the next few moves.

7.a4 Clever to start with this and not play 7.c3 d6 first, because then 8.a4 would also allow the option of 8...♗g4.

7...♖b8 8.c3 Durarbayli, who is a very experienced and very strong grandmaster with an excellent track record, went for the 8.♘xe5 variation.

8...d6 9.d4 ♗b6

10.a5 The point is that 10...♘xa5? loses to 11.♖xa5! ♗xa5 12.dxe5!, while if Black goes 10...♗a7, he'll have to deal with some tactics after 11.h3 0-0 12.♗e3, since the a7-bishop is badly protected.

10...♗a7 11.h3 ♗b7 The latest trend, intending to go for direct complications with 12.♗e3 ♘xe4!?.

12.♗e3 White could also start with 12.♖e1, as Harikrishna played against Caruana in Wijk aan Zee this year.

12...♘xe4 As said, this is the point.

13.d5 The most direct test, but

13.♖e1 has been played here, too.

13...♗xe3 14.dxc6

14...♘xf2 Forced complications.

15.♕e2 The consensus is that this is the best. **15...♘xh3+ 16.♔h1 ♘f2+ 17.♖xf2 ♗xf2** And here White is at a principled crossroads. There are two attempts, because there are two bishops that can be captured.

18.♕xf2!? 18.cxb7 ♗a7 is my game against Grischuk, and a few prepared moves down the line he repeated: 19.♗d5 ♕d7 20.♘d4 ♕e7 21.♗c6+ ♔f8 22.♘f3 d5 23.♕xe5 ♕xe5 24.♘xe5 ♔e7 25.♗xb5 axb5 26.a6 ♔d6 27.♘xf7+ ♔c6 28.♘e5+ ♔d6 29.♘f7+ ♔c6 30.♘e5+ ♔d6 31.♘f7+ ½-½, Grischuk-Giri, Zagreb 2021.

18...♗xc6 19.♘xe5

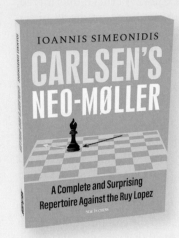

19...⌗xg2+! A crucial intermezzo, intending to throw out the d8-queen with a check. **20.⌗g1!** Forced as well. Now Black has no checks left.

20...⌗f6 After the game JKD said that he had expected Vidit to follow a correspondence game with 20...0-0, which leads to a draw. There seems to be nothing wrong with Vidit's solution either.

After 20...0-0!? 21.♘xf7 ⌗e7 22.♘d2, Black has to know a couple of important moves to reach the desired 0.00: 22...d5! 23.⌗xg2 ⌗e3+ 24.⌗h1 ⌗xf7!!, and the complications end in a draw. Stuff that's impossible to find, but can be memorized.

21.♘xf7

The best. Now we reach an endgame by force. **21...⌗xf2+ 22.⌗xf2 ⌗f8 23.⌗xg2 ⌗xf7 24.⌗xf7+ ⌗xf7** This is the endgame both players had been going for. White has a knight for three pawns, which is fine material compensation for Black, but he does have to watch out a bit, since the a6-pawn is fixed by the a5-pawn and Black would be under pressure if the knight ever landed on b4. But that would never happen... or would it?

25.♘d2

25...⌗e8
I didn't like this particular solution, although it is not a bad move objectively. It felt more practical to include 25...b4 26.c4, get counterplay with ...⌗e8-e5, or go for 25...g5!?, giving the king a nice square on g6 behind the pawns instead of in front of them.

26.⌗f1+ An annoying check.

26...⌗g6 Allowing the rook trade and going for a very concrete knight vs pawn ending is not something you want to be dealing with this early in the game, but now the king is somewhat awkwardly placed in front of its pawns.

27.⌗f2! Strong. The g-file is free for the rook and the king takes it upon himself to stop the invasion of the rook.

27...h5 Black wants to start pushing his kingside pawns.

28.⌗g1+ ⌗f6 29.⌗f3!?
29.♘f3 may seem automatic at first, but this is a far more clever way to stop the pawns, intending ♘e4+.

29...g6 30.♘e4+ ⌗g7

31.♘f2! Duda makes one nasty move after the other. Here I already started feeling the heat for Vidit, but

the engine still pointed out a clear-cut solution – 31...⌗h6! 32.♘d3 g5!.

31...⌗f8+?! Fishing for move repetition is tempting, but it won't yield Black the desired result.

32.⌗g2

32...⌗e8?
Continuing with the wrong plan. White isn't forced to take the draw and this only gives him more time. Keeping control of the f4-square was much better, with the immediate 32...⌗f5 or first 32...⌗f4 33.⌗a1 ⌗f5 34.♘d3 c5, and Black manages to keep the knight at bay and wants to start pushing his kingside. The position is still very drawish.

33.♘d3!

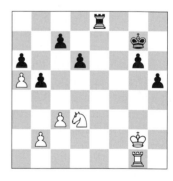

Now Black is suddenly in serious trouble. He has to allow either ♘b4 or ♘f4.

33...g5
Correct, as 33...c5 34.♘f4! was losing, with ⌗f3 coming next and Black's kingside pawns unable to move.

34.♘b4
Black has to answer some very hard questions, but objectively this seems to be still within the drawing margins.

34...♖e2+? Very tempting, but Vidit had missed JKD's strong sequence. Instead, 34...c5! leads to a defensible position. Black gives up a pawn, but gets rid of the main issue, the passed a5-pawn: 35.♘xa6 ♖a8 36.♘c7 ♖xa5, and Black holds: 37.♘e8+ (there are also other tries) 37...♔g6 38.♘xd6 ♖a2 39.♖b1 b4 40.c4 b3

As Jan-Krzysztof Duda destroyed Vidit Gujrathi's dreams, he began to realize that his spot in the semi-finals guaranteed his participation in the Candidates.

ANALYSIS DIAGRAM

and Black is apparently OK, since he can combine the relative instability of White's queenside pawns with the advance of his own kingside soldiers. This wasn't easy, but it had to be done, because the game move loses by force. **35.♔h1!**

The king is no longer in danger of any checks, neither by the pawns nor by the rook. A very aesthetically pleasing solution.

35...♖xb2 36.♖a1! Grabbing the a-file before collecting the a6-pawn. The a5-pawn is now unstoppable. Note that with the king on f3 Black would have counterplay thanks to ...g4+ and ...♖b3xc3, check, but with the king on h1, his counterplay is far too slow.

36...c5 37.♘xa6 b4 A last-ditch attempt, but JKD is merciless.

38.♘xb4! This leads to a major-piece endgame in which White gets to check first and Black's king has nowhere to hide. **38...cxb4 39.a6 bxc3 40.a7 c2 41.a8♕ ♖b1+ 42.♔g2 c1♕**
Now White starts giving checks, and the enemy king ends up getting mated.

43.♖a7+ ♔f6 44.♕f8+ ♔e5
45.♖e7+ ♔d5 46.♕f3+ ♔c5
47.♖c7+ ♔b4 48.♕b7+ ♔a5
49.♕a7+ ♔b5 50.♕b8+

Black resigned. A crucial win for the eventual World Cup winner.

Karjakin again

Although he had played well so far and reached the semi-finals, Magnus Carlsen must have felt that he had, in fact, not accomplished anything yet. For the World Champion the only prize that mattered was the $110,000 first prize. For all the others it is safe to say that a spot in the Candidates tournament was the main objective. As, according to the rules, Carlsen could not claim one of the two available spots in the Candidates because of his participation in the upcoming World Championship match, they were to be divided between the other semi-finalists Karjakin, Fedoseev and Duda. Besides this issue, the last four would obviously also decide how the prizes would be split.

No one doubts that Sergey Karjakin is a special player with unusual talents, and one of them is to excel when there is more than money alone at stake. His road had perhaps been bumpy, but he was one of the last four standing, and after he knocked out his compatriot Vladimir Fedoseev in the following game, Karjakin was the first to reach the final.

NOTES BY
Anish Giri

Sergey Karjakin
Vladimir Fedoseev
Sochi World Cup 2021 (7.2)
Ruy Lopez, Zaitsev Variation

1.e4 e5 2.♘f3 ♘c6 3.♗b5 a6 4.♗a4 ♘f6 5.0-0 ♗e7 6.♖e1 b5 7.♗b3 d6 8.c3 0-0 9.h3 ♗b7
Vladimir Fedoseev sticks to the complex and rich Zaitsev Variation of the Ruy Lopez that he had played previously in the event as well. There are more solid options available for the second game of a mini-match, but Vladimir stays true to his uncompromising style and is inviting a fight.

10.d4 ♖e8 11.♘bd2 ♗f8
The main idea of the Zaitsev Variation is to prevent the desired ♘f1-g3 regrouping and thus hinder the development of the c1-bishop.
12.a3 This subtle move order is not new. White is waiting to see what Black has to say and prepares ♗c2, followed by ♘f1, now that the b4-square has been taken under control and ...exd4 cxd4 ♘b4 will

not be an issue. At the same time, compared to starting with 12.♗c2, White is keeping his options open and may now go for ♗a2!? instead.

12...h6 The alternative is 12...g6!?, but this is the main move.

13.♗c2 Now White is ready for the ♘f1-g3 manoeuvre, and Black has to address that.

13...d5!?

The main move here is the Breyer-style 13...♘b8!?, which would prevent ♘f1. White then usually develops his c1-bishop to b2, after b3 or b4, and we get a long slow game. Vladimir shows, once again, that he wants to steer the game towards more complex positions.

The central pawn break is not new either and has been played, by, amongst others, Vidit, who certainly wouldn't play a messy move like that without doing his homework.

14.dxe5 White has to clarify the situation in the centre.

14...♘xe5 15.♘xe5 ♖xe5 16.♘f3

16...♖e8

Sacrificing the exchange on e4 has been tried a couple of times, but it is probably not completely sound.

Who wouldn't jump for joy? Making it to the Candidates, Sergey Karjakin once again demonstrated that qualifying competitions bring the best out in him.

17.e5 ♘e4

Now we get an interesting pawn structure, reminiscent of the Open Spanish Variation. Both players seemed to be well prepared so far.

18.♗f4 c5 19.a4 f5

The main move, following Oparin-Morozevich 2015 and the more recent Tari-Vidit 2018. Now, suddenly, Sergey Karjakin went into deep thought.

20.h4!?

An interesting new move, probably improvised. Tari-Vidit went down the more forcing path with 20.♘d2 ♕h4!.

20...♗e7 21.h5

White grabs some squares and would get a dominant position if he were to send the f3-knight miraculously towards the g6-square. This should have been a warning sign for Fedoseev, but he erred quickly.

21...♖f8? This allows a painful shot. The text-move is a huge mistake that pretty much costs Vladimir the game – unsurprisingly, since positions as strategically complex as this one don't leave too much room for mistakes. Live by the sword, die by the sword.

21...♕b6!? was stronger, taking control of the e6-square and intending ...♖ad8.

22.axb5 A good inclusion, getting rid of some irrelevant pieces.

22...axb5 23.♖xa8 ♗xa8

24.e6! Clearing the path for the much desired ♘e5-g6. To make matters worse, the rook on f8 now will have to lose a tempo. Black is in deep trouble and fails to put up a fight any longer.

24...♖e8 25.♘e5! Sending the knight to g6. The e6-pawn will be indirectly protected.

25...♗g5 26.♘g6!

The knight is brilliantly positioned here. f2-f3 is now a possibility as well.

26...d4

Fedoseev goes for the mess, but it just doesn't work and Karjakin calmly calculates everything.

26...♖xe6 is losing: 27.♗xg5 (it is accurate to start with this move). Now taking with the knight gives up the f5-pawn and invites disaster along the e-file, while taking with the queen loses material: 27...♕xg5 28.f3!

ANALYSIS DIAGRAM

and the tactics work: 28...♕xh5 29.♘f4! ♕h4 30.♗xe4! (the last important detail) 30...♕xf4 31.♗xd5, winning a full rook on the pin.

27.cxd4 ♘xf2 Desperation.

28.♔xf2 ♗xf4 29.♘xf4 ♕h4+

30.♔g1! Very clean. White returns the piece, but with the connected pawns storming down the centre of the board, there is no salvation.

30...♕xf4 31.d5! ♕g3 Blocking with 31...♕d6 doesn't help: 32.♗xf5 ♕xd5 33.♕xd5 ♗xd5 34.e7, winning material.

32.♖e2 ♕g5 33.♕d2!

Again the cleanest. The pawns are unstoppable and there is zero counter-play left. Black was forced to resign.

Absolute highlight

In the interview in this issue, Jan-Krzysztof Duda shares his thoughts on his rapid win against Magnus Carlsen that he views as an absolute high point in his career. But he insisted on providing his technical comments (and more insights) as well.

NOTES BY
Jan-Krzysztof Duda

Magnus Carlsen
Jan-Krzysztof Duda
Sochi World Cup 2021 (7.4)
Sicilian Defence, Moscow Variation

Playing Black in the second rapid game wasn't a rosy prospect, taking into account that, before Sochi, I had garnered a terrible score against Magnus as Black: ½ out of 5 (which I improved after the first classical game by a respectable 6.6%).

So making a draw, and trying to make it to the next stage of the match – two more rapid games – was the main aim.

1.e4 c5 2.♘f3 d6 3.♗b5+

Magnus might play any opening at top-level quality, but somehow we had guessed correctly that this check, the so-called Moscow Variation, was likely to happen. It's of totally no relevance that Magnus had played it in the World Cup before, against Wojtaszek and Bacrot respectively ☺.

3...♗d7 4.♗xd7+ ♕xd7

Recently, I had toyed more with

4...♘xd7, but against certain systems the knight might be misplaced there. This is definitely the case against the c3/d4 set-up, as in the game Carlsen-Xiong, Clutch Championship 2020. My choice is better suited to counter it, but the World Champion still went for this option.

5.0-0 ♘f6

6.♕e2 Interestingly, I have always regarded this move as leading to rather drawish positions. 6.♖e1 is a far more challenging option, since it would allow White to deploy both his rooks along the third rank to attack the black monarch. Of course, Magnus wasn't content with an easy draw, and it was clear that he had prepared a practical idea.

6...♘c6 7.c3 7.♖d1 is another option, played by Gallagher against me at the Tromsø Olympiad 2014. Amongst other things, Black can consider playing 7...g5!? here.

7...e6 8.d4 cxd4 9.cxd4 d5 10.e5 ♘e4 11.♘bd2 Here, 11.♗e3 is the most common white move, intending to get a super-solid game.

11...♘xd2 12.♗xd2 ♗b4!?

I didn't know any games played in this exact position, and decided to blitz out this rather unexpected move. On paper, my bishop should be preferable to its white colleague, but, with less space, exchanges should normally favour Black.

13.♗f4

And Magnus decided against trading bishops, which is a novelty. Now the manoeuvring phase of the game begins, with both players trying to make progress on their flanks.

13...0-0 14.♕d3 ♗e7 15.a3 ♖ac8 16.g3 I expected him to be more direct with a 'Harry the h-pawn' march. The truth is that it is not all that scary for Black, provided he doesn't allow the pawn to reach h6.

16...♘a5

16...a5!? 17.h4 ♘a7, with the idea of ...♕b5, was another viable plan.

17.b3 ♕c6

After 17...a6, 18.♗d2 would have affected my coordination somewhat.

18.♗d2 ♕b6

19.♖fb1

19.♖fd1 deserved attention, indirectly protecting the b3-pawn and trying to save a tempo. However, Black might have even considered the Lasker queen sac, either at once or, even better, after some preparation, with 19...♘xb3!? 20.♖ab1 ♘xd2 21.♖xb6 ♘xf3+ 22.♕xf3 axb6, with a roughly equal position.

19...a6 20.♔g2 ♘c6 21.♖e1 Freeing the b1-square for his queen, which I believe is the only way to present Black with some challenges. The engines prefer 21.h4, but 21...♕b5 22.♕e3 ♖c7 23.♖c1 ♖fc8 looks harmless.

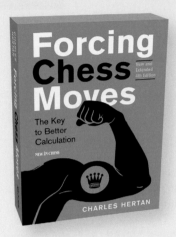

Lothar Schmid: 'When you are young, chess is a sport and you play to win. Now that I am older, my interests have changed, but I love the game as much or more through my book collection.' *(The German GM, fabled arbiter and legendary book collector, at the 1988 Chess Collectors International convention in Munich)*

Rafael Benitez: 'But I want to win. It doesn't matter what competition, I just want to win. That's the same with any game. If I play chess with my daughter, my wife is telling me, "Listen, why don't you allow her to win?" That's just how I am.' *(The Everton manager, speaking to the media ahead of the new English Premier League season)*

Tylor Glasnow: 'I used to live down there in the offseason. I was there for like parts of three years. So, I was in like Chelsea in the West Village, so I'm kind of familiar with that area. And I would just go to the park and get beat by all the chess players, but it was still fun.' *(The Tampa Bay Rays World Series-winning pitcher's answer to a journalist, on being photographed in early June playing chess with the street hustlers in Washington Square Park after pitching seven innings against the New York Yankees the night before)*

Hou Yifan: 'Most girls are told at an early age that there's a kind of gender distinction, and they should just try their best in the girls' section and be happy with that. So, without the motivation to chase higher goals, it's harder for some girls to improve as fast as boys as they grow up.' *(Interviewed by New Yorker staff writer Louisa Thomas, in the August issue feature 'Queenside', that explores the wait for chess's first woman world champion)*

Ellen Carlsen: 'I don't think I have ever felt intellectually inferior to any of the guys I played against. I think to most people it is clear that your chess rating is not identical to your intellectual abilities.' *(The world champion's sister, in the same New Yorker feature)*

Mikhail Botvinnik: 'Chess is a socialistic game, the pieces are people who work together for a common goal.'

Henrik Carlsen: 'Whether he was thinking about chess or reading Donald Duck, he [Magnus] was using the same playful approach, using his intuition, his curiosity.' *(The World Champion's father, on watching the development of his son as he grew up with chess)*

Alex Yermolinsky: 'When I was 20 years old, it was more like a matter of life and death playing chess. Now it's a different perspective, but I know I will enjoy playing those guys.' *(Interviewed by The Argus Leader on what motivates him to still play chess, on the eve of the US Senior Championship)*

Grigory Sanakoev: 'There are no hopeless positions; there are only inferior positions that can be saved. There are no drawn positions; there are only equal ones in which you can play for a win. But at the same time, don't forget that there is no such thing as a won position in which it is impossible to lose.' *(The 12th World Correspondence Champion, in his book World Champion at the Third Attempt)*

Enid Blyton: 'When I was six my father taught me to play draughts, and a little later he taught me to play chess. That was just before I was seven. He thought that all young children should learn to play chess. "If they have any brains it will train them to think clearly, quickly and to plan things a long way ahead", he said. "And if they haven't any brains it will make the best of those they have!" I don't know if he was right. I know that I enjoyed the games immensely.' *(The legendary children's author, in her 1952 autobiography, The Story of My Life)*

Mig Greengard: 'Do we really remember anything Dvoretsky, Nunn, and Pandolfini have to say while we're actually playing? Hell, I'm lucky to remember how to spell Dvoretsky, let alone recall the "rule of eighteen weaknesses" until I already have seventeen in my position.'

21...♕b5

During the game I believed that expelling the white lady from d3 was a major achievement. The d4-pawn requires constant protection now, making it harder for White to unleash an attack on my king. For example, the annoying jump ♘g5 is impossible now.

22.♕b1 ♖c7

22...a5 23.h4 a4 at once would obviously also have been good. There is nothing wrong with doubling the rooks on the c-file first, in particular because Magnus started playing a bit more timidly from here on in.

23.h4 ♖fc8 24.♖a2

24.h5 h6 25.g4 was again more direct, but Black is OK after 25...a5, starting his own counterplay.

24...a5 25.♖h1 a4

26.b4? Objectively a bad move from a positional viewpoint, but it was a clear sign that Magnus didn't care about his queenside – he just wanted to checkmate me!

26...h6 27.♗e3?

Quite an odd move, I must confess. I guess the World Champion have missed something very basic, as he played the bishop back on the next move. Still, Black is objectively better after other White tries.

I felt uneasy about 27.♘g5?, at various points in the game, but I guess it was just because I had seen too many pawn phalanxes rolling in my life. In reality, it never really worked for White, and it doesn't here: 27...hxg5 28.hxg5 g6 29.♖h6 ♗f8 30.♖xg6+ fxg6 31.♕xg6+ ♗g7 32.♕xe6+ ♔f8 33.♕f5+ ♔e8 34.♕g6+ ♔d8, and Black is winning.

And of course 27.g4 was begging to be played. It's very interesting that Magnus refrained from it throughout the game, only going for it when he had (almost) run out of other options. There is only one way to be better, but I think I would have been able to deal with it, as I played similarly in the game: 27...♘a7 28.h5 (28.g5 h5 29.g6 ♕e8! is nearly winning for Black) 28...♕e2! 29.♖e1 ♕a6 30.g5 ♘b5!, and the computer screams that Black is better.

27...♘a7 28.♗d2 ♕e2!

A nice move to play, and a strong one indeed, although there was nothing wrong with the immediate 28...♕a6.

29.♖e1

29.♗xh6 won't work: 29...♖c2 30.♖xc2 ♖xc2 31.♗e3 ♘b5!, and Black's position looks great. Yet, I was surprised to learn it's actually –6!

29...♖c4?

A bad concept. I was aware of the fact that the queen is not supposed to occupy the file before the rooks, but the pressure against the d4-pawn, alongside with the tempting ...♕b3 jumps, made me think differently. In fact, the plan is so bad that I should have withdrawn the queen whenever the chance occurred in the next couple of moves.

After 29...♕a6! Black is a lot better, e.g. 30.♖e3 ♘b5 31.♕d1 ♖c4 32.♖d3 ♗d8, with ...♗b6 and ♕a7 in mind (32...♔f8!? 33.♖b2 ♔e8 would have been even classier).

30.♖e3 ♘b5 31.♖d3 ♖c6

With the sophisticated ...♗d8-b6 manoeuvre in mind, after which I thought I was about to get some new entry squares. Almost true, but I had missed an important detail.

COLOPHON

PUBLISHER: Remmelt Otten
EDITOR-IN-CHIEF:
Dirk Jan ten Geuzendam
HONORARY EDITOR: Jan Timman
CONTRIBUTING EDITOR: Anish Giri
EDITORS: Peter Boel, René Olthof
PRODUCTION: Joop de Groot
TRANSLATOR: Piet Verhagen
SALES AND ADVERTISING: Edwin van Haastert
PHOTOS AND ILLUSTRATIONS IN THIS ISSUE:
Øystein Brekke, Maria Emelianova, FIDE, Atle Grønn,
Lennart Ootes, Eric Rosen, David Llada, Studiocanal/
Walker+Worm Film/Julia Terjung, Berend Vonk
COVER PHOTO: Maria Emelianova
COVER DESIGN: Hélène Bergmans

© No part of this magazine may be reproduced,
stored in a retrieval system or transmitted in any
form or by any means, recording or otherwise,
without the prior permission of the publisher.

NEW IN CHESS
P.O. BOX 1093
1810 KB ALKMAAR
THE NETHERLANDS

PHONE: 00-31-(0)72-51 27 137
SUBSCRIPTIONS: nic@newinchess.com
EDITORS: editors@newinchess.com

WWW.NEWINCHESS.COM

32.♖b2 ♗d8 33.g4? It's a tragicomedy that out of two sensible moves, Magnus decided to go for this pawn push only now. 33.♕f1! was very strong, because after 33...♗b6 he can basically make a draw with 34.♖b1!, and suddenly there is no way to stop the harassment of Black's queen by means of ♖c1/♖a1/♖b1, etc.
33...♗b6

Now I'm much better again.
34.♗e3 ♘c3 35.♕f1 ♕b5 36.♖c2 ♘e4?!
Just missing a trick; otherwise I would have chosen one of the following options, 36...♕a6 or 36...♗d8.

37.♖xc6? From now on, strange things are going to happen in this nerve-wracking encounter. This was one of the most bizarre moments in my career, when my strong rival was thinking for some period of time, and I had literally no idea why – there was only ♖xc6 and nothing else, wasn't there? Needless to say, I had completely missed the nasty ♖c5, after which the nature of the game would have changed drastically, making it extremely tactical. Luckily for me, Magnus didn't like

what he saw, burning some time in the process.
After 37.♖c5! ♗xc5 38.dxc5 all my pieces are kind of ridiculous, but the extra exchange and the somewhat exposed position of the white monarch still make my position preferable.
37...♖xc6 38.♕d1? White's position was critical, but trading queens was hardly the way to go.
After 38.♕d1 Black is lord and master, but White is in no way finished here.

38...♖c4?? Nonsense. I had been looking to trade queens the entire game, and, now having the chance, I declined ☺. I had my reasons, of course, but this just lacked sense.
In fact, 38...♕xf1+ was winning on the spot: 39.♖xf1 ♖c3 40.♖c1 (after 40.♖a1 ♖b3 41.h5 ♔h7, with ...g5 coming next, Black will lock down the kingside and win on the queenside) 40...♖xa3 41.♖c8+ ♔h7 42.♖b8. I stopped here, thinking 'with counterplay', forgetting about the possibility of 'mirroring' my opponent's last move with 42...♖b3!, and it would have been curtains after 43.♖xb7 ♖xb4.
39.♘d2 ♘xd2 40.♖xd2

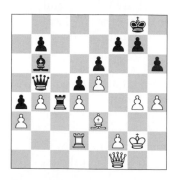

Trading knights was obviously sensible for White, and now he surely wants to start an offensive on the kingside. I definitely could have played better at this stage, but let's not forget it was a rapid game, and this was the prelude to a time-scramble.
40...♕c6 41.♕e2 ♖c3? Actually a mistake. I should have had something concrete in store against White's g5 ! 41...♖c1 was significantly stronger, because now the g5-push is just bad: 42.g5? hxg5 43.hxg5 ♕c4, and Black is winning.

42.♖a2?? An inexplicable error; one more for the collection of weird moves. For better or worse, White should have gone for 42.g5, which is good enough for equality: 42...hxg5 43.hxg5 ♕c4 44.♕g4 ♖c1 45.♖d1 ♖xd1 46.♕xd1, and the endgame is OK for White.
42...♗d8!? Sophisticated. There was nothing wrong with the natural 42...♕c4, when Black is about to get a winning endgame, but I had a dream of an improved version with White's kingside pawns being shattered.
43.g5

Grist to my mill. Now White is no longer able to create any counterplay on the kingside, so perhaps other pawn moves would have been a bit more tenacious.

43...hxg5 44.hxg5 ♛c4 After trading queens it should have been a simple matter of technique, but given the prize at stake and the time-trouble it was an anything but effortless win. **45.♛xc4**

Magnus Carlsen ends a dramatic roller-coaster by congratulating Jan- Krzysztof Duda on his place in the World Cup final.

45...dxc4 I must confess I was frustrated with myself after making this move. Why on earth not listen to your first instinct, recapture with the rook, and win without any ado? After 45...♖xc4 it is just game over, with three weaknesses in White's camp, and a nice king march via h7 and g6.
46.d5 exd5 47.♖d2
Here, having the World Champion on the ropes, and with about one minute on the clock – which should be more than enough – I suddenly blanked.

47...♖d3? 47...♖xa3 was a ridiculously easy win: 48.♖xd5 ♖d3 49.♖c5 a3, but here I got some incomprehensible delusions, like White generating some counterplay by means of g6 or e6, which in fact loses instantly to ...a2, and after 50.♖c8 ♔h7 there is not a single trick for White. I assume

it was a combination of fatigue and my constant desire to not allow counterplay throughout the game.
48.♖xd3 cxd3 49.f4
When I opted for 47...♖d3, I believed the bishop ending to be easily won. All White's pawns are on the dark squares, the a3-pawn is permanently weak and I'm a pawn up. Paradoxically, there is only one move to win here, which I didn't consider at all.

49...♔f8? Letting the win slip. 49...f6! was very important, to open inroads for both of my pieces. I was so fixed on the bad structure and bad bishop in White's camp that I think I was just unable to come up with such a solution.

50.♔f3? A mistake, as indicated by our silicon friend, because now Black is winning once again after ...f6!.
Both 50.♔f2 and 50.♔f1 were drawing, as White goes after the d3-pawn, keeping his bishop to eye the f4- and g5-pawns.
50...♔e7? 51.♗c5+ ♔e6 52.♔e3

Now White is suddenly in time, and it's a drawn endgame thanks to a small tactical trick that I had missed.
52...♔f5 53.♔xd3 g6 53...♔xf4?? 54.g6!, and suddenly White wins! From now on, it was kind of crazy, as we were just playing on increments, with me trying to win somehow.
54.♗e3 ♗c7

NEW IN CHESS bestsellers

Strategic Concepts, Typical Plans and Tactical Themes   *Oscar de Prado*

De Prado revisits his favourite opening. He avoids long and complicated variations and explains straightforward plans, clear-cut strategies and standard manoeuvres. If you follow his lessons you are unlikely to face surprises and you will learn to make the right middlegame choices. The most efficient way to acquaint yourself with an opening that is easy to learn and hard to counter.

Bobby Fischer's Road to Reykjavik
Jan Timman

How Fischer swept the field at the Palma Interzonal, crushed Taimanov, Larsen and Petrosian, while scoring an incredible 36 points from 43 games against many of the world's best players, including a streak of 19 consecutive wins.

"A delight to read."
Johannes Fischer, ChessBase News

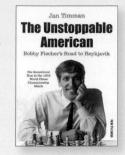

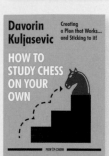

Creating a Plan that Works... and Sticking to It!
Davorin Kuljasevic

Stop wasting time and energy! Optimize your learning process, develop good study habits and get rid of useless ones.

"I recommend this book unconditionally, it will be the standard work on studying chess for years."
Barry Braeken, Schaaksite

"Extremely impressive."
Richard James, British Chess News

Start Playing an Unsidesteppable & Low Maintenance Response to 1.e4 and Simultaneously Improve Your Chess Technique
Thomas Willemze

"This is a real gem! It's almost as if each annotation specifies the key strategic elements that uphold the assessments and choice of plans. A repertoire apt for club players, offering lessons in strategy, plus antidotes to seemingly troublesome White tries."
GM Glenn Flear

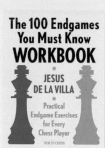

Practical Endgames Exercises for Every Chess Player
Jesus de la Villa

"I love this book! In order to master endgame principles you will need to practice them."
NM Han Schut, Chess.com

"The perfect supplement to De la Villa's manual. To gain sufficient knowledge of theoretical endgames you really only need two books."
IM Herman Grooten, Schaaksite

A Memoir of Players, Games and Engines
Larry Kaufman

The fascinating memoir of GM and former World Senior Champion, computer programmer and options trader, shogi player and bestselling chess author Larry Kaufman. Stories and anecdotes about dozens of famous and not-so-famous chess players. With lots of memorable but little-known annotated games.

"A riveting read." – *Richard James, British Chess News*

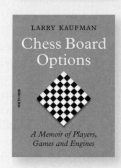

Fresh Strategies and Resources for Dynamic Chess Players   *Viktor Moskalenko*

Lots of original and dynamic options in every main line. A typical Moskalenko book: practical, accessible, original, entertaining and inspiring.

"You can hardly go wrong using this as your 'ideas source' for years to come." – *GM Glenn Flear*

"French players looking for new ideas or variations will find plenty of food for thought."
IM John Donaldson

Typical Structural and Strategic Manoeuvres
Boris Zlotnik

In 2004, 12-year-old Fabiano Caruana and his entire family moved to Madrid. The Caruanas wanted to be sure that Fabiano would be tutored by the best chess trainer in the world. And Madrid is where Boris Zlotnik lives.

"A brilliant, important and extraordinarily instructive book. I devoured it. A treasure trove for every club and tournament player."
Florian Jacobs, Max Euwe Center

A Practical Guide to a Vital Skill in Chess
Merijn van Delft

"Excellent examples. Will have a major impact on your positional progress."
IM Gary Lane, Chess Moves Magazine

"A grandmaster-level skill explained in a comprehensible and readable fashion."
GM Matthew Sadler

"Masterfully discusses a vital topic, to bring your chess to the next level." – *GM Karsten Müller*

A Complete, Sound and User-friendly Chess Opening Repertoire   *Larry Kaufman*

"His recommendations are well-conceived, and I was impressed with how much Kaufman was able to stuff into these pages."
John Hartmann, Chess Life

"Kaufman does an outstanding job."
IM Gary Lane

"A good starting point for anyone wanting to give their openings a major overhaul."
CHESS Magazine

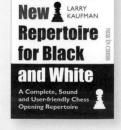

available at your local (chess)bookseller or at www.newinchess.com

55.b5

This felt risky to me, as now the a3-f8 diagonal is opened, and it's easier to get to the a3-pawn. Still the move is perfectly OK.

55.♗c5!? is a nasty trick, as Black can't take 55...♔xf4?? in view of 56.♗d6, and White wins.

55...♗d8 56.♔d4 ♗b6+ 57.♔d3 ♗d8 58.♔d4 ♗e7 59.♗c1 ♔e6 60.♗b2 After some neutral moves, we came to a position in which I had a decent try.

60...♗d8

Obviously, it was not easy to put my b-pawn on a dark square, but after 60...b6!? White would have had to find three only moves in order not to lose: 61.♔d3! ♗c5 62.♗d4! ♗xa3 63.♔c2!, and White regains the pawn, with equality, as the pawn ending is not an option for Black: 63...♗c5?? 64.♗xc5 bxc5 65.b6 ♔d7 66.f5, winning.

61.♔c5 ♗a5 62.♗c1??

I think it's a natural instinct to defend both vulnerable pawns in one go, but this is, in fact, a losing blunder, which with some luck I managed to exploit. 62.♗d4! was the only move to draw, which I think we both failed to see.

62...♗c3! Probably my best move of the game, but played with a wrong idea in mind. Only after making it did I realize how strong it actually was. So, one can argue that I won the game because of luck, and I agree that this is actually true about the bishop ending. But thinking in such terms also reveals that the fact that this endgame occurred was extremely unlucky ☺. On a serious note, even the best players in the history of chess make mistakes after having been pressed for a long time, and I believe that this

Sochi World Cup 2021	
8 rounds of knock-out	
Eighth Finals	
Carlsen-Esipenko	5-3
Bacrot-Piorun	4-2
Duda-Grischuk	2½-1½
Vidit-Durarbayli	1½-½
Fedoseev-Ilic	3-1
Tabatabaei-Martirosyan	2½-1½
Karjakin-Vachier-Lagrave	3½-2½
Shankland-Svidler	1½-½
Quarter Finals	
Carlsen-Bacrot	2-0
Duda-Vidit	1½-½
Fedoseev-Tabatabaei	1½-½
Karjakin-Shankland	4-2
Semi-Finals	
Duda-Carlsen	2½-1½
Karjakin-Fedoseev	1½-½
Final 3rd/4th place	
Carlsen-Fedoseev	2-0
Final 1st/2nd place	
Duda-Karjakin	1½-½

is the main reason for my victory in the match against Magnus and of the World Cup in general.

63.b6 d4 64.♔c4 ♔d7

This doesn't spoil anything, but the king should have gone the other way, when after 64...♔f5 65.♔d3, 65...♗a1! is a nice zugzwang move.

65.♗e3 A decent trick, but, I was too biased towards the quality of the bishops to consider exchanging them.

65...♗b2 Now at last there is no longer a way to spoil the position. White has too many weaknesses to keep his position together.

Of course not 65...dxe3?? 66.♔xc3, and White is even winning.

66.♗xd4 ♗xa3 67.♗e3 ♗b2 68.♔b4 a3 69.♔b3 ♔e6 70.♗a2 ♔d5 71.♔b3 ♔e4 72.♗d2

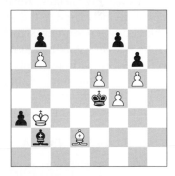

72...♗d4 73.♔xa3 ♗xb6 74.♔b4 ♗f2 White resigned.

An interesting game, not immune to mistakes or even gross errors, but a nice fighting clash. Taking into account the strength of my opponent, and the stakes I was facing, I think it's my biggest chess accomplishment ever, and definitely a fruitful experience for the future.

After three weeks, the Final!

The final days of the Sochi World Cup were unique in that it wasn't only the fight for the trophy that was exciting to follow, but that in the shadow of that clash, Magnus Carlsen showed his extra class. His two brilliancies against Fedoseev you will find in a separate article. We round off these impressions with the decisive game of the 2021 World Cup with insightful comments by the winner, Jan-Krzysztof Duda.

NOTES BY
Jan-Krzysztof Duda

Jan-Krzysztof Duda
Sergey Karjakin
Sochi World Cup 2021 (8.2)
Queen's Gambit Declined, Semi-Tarrasch

After a short draw in the first game, I was having the comfortable advantage of the white pieces. I was fully aware that no matter what, it was never going to be easy, because Sergey Karjakin has his 'Minister of Defence' nickname for a reason, and, also because he had far more experience in such 'big clashes'. Both of us were extremely tired, but Sergey had had tougher moments in his previous matches, having been on the verge of elimination three times. So, making a long story short, it was basically a fight of age, experience and fatigue – two of which were favouring me ☺.
1.d4 ♘f6 2.c4 e6 3.♘f3 d5 4.♘c3 c5

I hadn't expected the Semi-Tarrasch, even though Sergey had played it in his previous match against Vladimir Fedoseev. I had anticipated him to rely on his beloved QGD, an even more solid opening, in this key game.
5.cxd5 cxd4 6.♕xd4 exd5 7.♗g5 ♗e7 8.e3 0-0

9.♖d1
I couldn't recall my analysis and had played 9.♗d3 against Alexander Grischuk earlier in the tournament, but it seems to be the least favourable move order for White. Small wonder, then, that after 9...h6 10.♗h4 ♘c6 11.♕a4 my opponent, who is an opening connoisseur, came up with the novel 11...♗d7!?, which is a good equalizer. I even had it as good for Black in my notes.
11...♗e6 12.♖d1 ♕b6 13.♖d2 was my idea for the game, as in Wojtaszek-Van Foreest, Wijk aan Zee 2021, with the tiniest of edges for White (½-½, 40).
Now, after 11...♗d7, I played 12.♕d1?! (12.0-0 ♘e5 13.♗b5 ♘xf3+ 14.gxf3 ♗e6 is very much OK for Black, although 14...♗h3!? 15.♖fd1 ♘e4 is even better),

ANALYSIS DIAGRAM

a dubious OTB improvisation. 12...♗g4 13.h3 ♗xf3 14.♕xf3 d4 15.♗xf6 ♗xf6 16.♘d5 and here, instead of 16...♗g5 (½-½, 28), 16...♕a5+ 17.♔f1 ♗e5!, with the initiative for Black, would have been better.
9...♘c6 10.♕a4 ♗e6

11.♗b5
Here, I decided to change plans and see how well Sergey was prepared. My first idea was to transpose to the game Wojtaszek-Van Foreest with 11.♗d3.
11...♕b6?!
Actually a serious inaccuracy. I remembered analysing 11...♖c8, and that after 12.♗xc6 Black can recapture in both ways (White can also play 12.0-0, of course) – 12...bxc6 or 12...♖xc6 13.♕xa7 ♖c8 14.0-0 ♗g4, with compensation for the pawn.

12.♗xf6!
It wasn't particularly difficult to play this move, since a few more moves give White an easy advantage. A clear improvement over Anish Giri's 12.0-0 a6 13.♗xc6 bxc6 14.♕c2 (1-0, 55, Giri-Wang Yue, Beijing 2011), when Black has easy play with 14...♖ac8 or 14...♗g4.

Now I got a dream scenario with a comfortable advantage, for two results only. Even the headache that I was beginning to feel around this time couldn't stop me that day ☺.

12...♗xf6 13.♘xd5 ♗xd5 14.♖xd5 ♗xb2 15.♔e2!?

A nice move, keeping the king in the centre, so that it'll be much stronger in the potential endgame. I couldn't see any variation in which my king would be in any real danger with the queens on. But it seems that orthodox castling would have been better nevertheless.

15...♗f6

Of course it was important that he could not swipe all the rooks off the board: 15...♖ad8 16.♖hd1 ♖xd5 17.♖xd5 ♖d8? 18.♗xc6 bxc6 19.♕xa7, and White wins.

15...a6 is not much of an improvement either: 16.♗xc6 bxc6 17.♕a5!? ♕b7 18.♖c5, with a strong initiative.

16.♖hd1 ♖ac8

Surprisingly, 16...h6! is the best move in the position. Black makes a useful move and waits for White to play, intending to tailor his play to White's move, for instance 17.♗c4 ♖ad8, and White is only marginally better.

Jan-Krzysztof Duda knows that he is very close to winning the World Cup, and Sergey Karjakin knows it, too.

17.♗c4!

A nice idea, eyeing f7, and keeping his options open. Move by move Black's position is starting to collapse.

17...♕b4?!

The trade of queens makes White's play extremely easy, and doesn't bring any relief for Black. It must be said, though, that White is better, no matter what Black does, and it's a thankless task to choose between bad and worse.

After 17...a6 18.♖d7 ♘b8 19.♖7d6 White is clearly better.

17...♘a5 at least makes me choose. I remember not being sure how to proceed exactly, but after 18.♖xa5 ♖xc4 19.♕xc4 ♕xa5 20.♖d7 b5 21.♕d5 White has a dominant position.

17...♖fd8 is the most obvious continuation, but it requires some only moves from Black to stay afloat: 18.♖d7 (of course 18.g4, avoiding concrete variations, is also fine) 18...♕b2+ 19.♔f1 ♖xd7! 20.♖xd7 ♕b1+ 21.♔e2 ♕b2+! 22.♘d2 ♘e5 (all forced for Black) 23.♖c7 ♖d8 24.♗d5 ♘c6 25.♕e4, and White is much better. All these

lines are a good indication of how tough Black's position has suddenly become.

18.♕b3! ♕xb3 19.♗xb3

White's pieces are clearly superior to Black's, and there is no way to stop the snowball effect on the kingside.

It was basically a fight of age, experience and fatigue – two of which were favouring me

Not only is Black's defence now desperate, but White also has several plausible continuations.

19...♘b8 20.g4

20...h6

This move creates additional motifs along the h-file and with the 'hanging' g6-pawn – although the Russian's future wouldn't be too bright either after other tries.

I thought that 20...g6 21.g5 ♗c3 22.h4 ♘a6 might have been more stubborn, but besides the h5-h6 push that I considered, there is another cunning little move: 23.♖c1 ♗g7 (23...♖c7?! 24.♘h2, unexpectedly, is completely winning for White, as he will set an unstoppable pawn phalanx in motion) 24.♖c4!, with a close to winning edge.

21.h4 g6

22.g5

22.h5 was another groovy possibility: 22...♔g7 (22...g5 23.♘d2, going for the juicy f5-square) 23.hxg6 fxg6 24.g5, and Black's position is extremely shaky.

22...hxg5 23.hxg5

23.h5!? was the coolest option, but one good way is enough.

23...♗e7 After 23...♗c3 there was a choice between 24.♘h4 and 24.♘h2, with the same core idea to reposition the knight and add more firepower to the attack.

24.♖e5 An ingenious idea, bringing the rook to e4, from where it can easily switch to the kingside. As they say, in a winning position everything works. 24.♘e5 ♔g7 25.f4 was also very strong.

24...♘c6 24...♗c5 would have prolonged the game somewhat, but it seems that White can win the f7-pawn almost by force, which must be decisive, e.g. 25.♖e4 ♔g7 26.♖h4 ♗e7 27.♖dh1 ♖h8 28.♖xh8 ♖xh8 29.♖xh8 ♔xh8 30.♗xf7 ♔g7 31.♗d5 b6 32.♔d3, and White is winning.

25.♖d7!

A flashy move, and strangely enough the only winning one.

I first thought that 25.♖e4 was winning as well, but miraculously Black can defend himself with 25...♖fd8 26.♖h1 ♗f8!, and from g7 the bishop will apparently hold the kingside together, e.g. 27.♘h2?! ♘a5 28.♘g4 ♗g7 29.♘f6+ ♔f8. But this is of no relevance, of course, since 25.♖d7 is much better and showier.

25...♗d8 To be honest, I had missed this defence. I even got a bit nervous at first, but my pieces are simply too active. The alternatives were 25...♘xe5 26.♘xe5 ♗g5, when both captures by the knight win handily, and after 25...♖fe8 26.♖e4 Black is in zugzwang.

26.♖b5 ♘a5?! 26...b6 would have been a bit more tenacious, but effectively it already no longer mattered.

27.♗d5 We had both forgotten about 27.♖xd8!, which is amusing, but also of no consequence whatever, since all roads were leading to Rome.

27...♖c7 28.♗xf7+ ♔g7 29.♖xc7 ♗xc7 30.♗d5

And Black resigned, making my biggest chess achievement come true.
Veni, vidi, vici, so to speak ☺. ∎

NICO ZWIRS:
THE FIANCHETTO SCANDINAVIAN (1.e4 d5 2.exd5 Nf6)

The Scandinavian is one of the most direct approaches against 1.e4. Right from the first move Black is attacking White's centre. A lot of players, especially club players, don't like to face this line because of this aggressive character. Most of them flee into offbeat lines which are not very critical. The ones who dare to go for the mainlines need to remember a lot of lines. This makes the Scandinavian a perfect choice for your repertoire. In the Fianchetto Scandinavian Dutch IM Nico Zwirs will share his experience with the love of his youth. The DVD will begin with an introduction, followed by starting with the main lines. The mainline from the repertoire will start with 1.e4 d5 2. exd5 Nf6 3.d4 Nxd5 4. c4 Nb6 5.Nf3 g6. From there on, the repertoire will be worked out backwards till the second move options for White.

The Fianchetto Scandinavian is characterised by the ...g6 ...Bg7 setup. From there on, Black will attack the centre, just as in the Grünfeld Defence. Where it is possible, Zwirs will fianchetto his bishop and explain the ideas. The plus side of this setup is that Black players are able to learn the repertoire by heart very easily. Of course, there are some cases where Black can't fianchetto his bishop and in those lines Zwirs explains why it's not a good idea and what the alternative is. Also, the viewer will learn about the dynamics of the opening. Normally one of the sides is going all out and sacrifices material or his pawn structure. In those cases it's important to know if you have to go all out or sit tight. In the end there is a bonus chapter where all the choices are explained, especially the reason why the repertoire isn't constructed around the Portuguese Gambit is interesting. This DVD is a must have for Scandinavian players or players looking for a new and creative opening. Video running time: 4 hours 25 min.

29,90 €

ROBERT RIS:
CALCULATION TRAINING IN ATTACK & DEFENCE VOL.1

Do I have to defend against my opponent's threat or can I simply ignore it and look for my own chances? A typical question which has often been asked during practical play. This two volume series on Calculation in Attack & Defence is the ideal guide to develop a good sense for attacking play, while keeping an eye on your opponent's defensive resources and possible counterplay against your own king. At the same time you'll be challenged to defend against your opponent's threats and, given the chance, turn the tables by launching a devastating counter-attack yourself. Video running time of Vol.1: more than 7 hours!

29,90 €

ROBERT RIS:
CALCULATION TRAINING IN ATTACK & DEFENCE VOL.2

The two DVDs offer you the chance to solve 66 exercises with multiple questions. These exercises are presented in the interactive format, which makes them accessible for players of different strengths as we will go through the thought process step by step and also explain why alternatives are not as good. All the examples are from games played in 2019 or later, which means a lot of new content you have not seen before. The ideal workout to further improve your tactical abilities and develop your sense for the initiative! Video running time of Vol.2: more than 7 hours!

29,90 €

Magnificent Encore

World Champion bids farewell to Sochi with two brilliancies

He had come to win, but his elimination in the semi-final did not put an end to Magnus Carlsen's ambitions. Still eager to show his very best, he defeated an equally audacious Vladimir Fedoseev 2-0 to claim third place. Carlsen's brilliant strangulation with Black in the first game won him the Gazprom beauty prize. The next day he conducted a masterful attack with the white pieces. It's a delight to relive the excitement of these two beauties with the expert commentary of **ANISH GIRI** and of Carlsen's coach **PETER HEINE NIELSEN.**

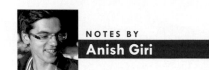

NOTES BY
Anish Giri

Vladimir Fedoseev
Magnus Carlsen
Sochi World Cup 2021
(Final 3rd/4th place, Game 1)
King's Indian Defence

1.d4 ♘f6 2.c4 g6 3.h4!?

Magnus Carlsen has gone for the Grünfeld (even less likely, a King's Indian), and Vladimir Fedoseev in his turn signals his readiness for a full-fledged fight. White has a ton of safer options, but no guts, no glory, and so 3.h4!? was essayed. The system had been a bit of a joke for a while, not least after Topalov played it against me in what was a terrible Candidates tournament for him in 2016, and it was only after Grischuk had reintroduced it in the 2019 Grand Prix that people realized that it was here to stay. The computers are surprisingly optimistic for White in the ensuing lines, but at the same time, Black can choose from a good King's Indian, a good Volga and a good Benoni.
3...♗g7 4.♘c3 d6 5.e4 ♘c6!?

A cunning move order by Magnus, played after some thinking. He was probably making a choice out of Black's many options. The idea of ...♘c6 this early is that Black is ready to strike with ...e5, while the usual d4-d5 push is slightly less of an issue, as we will see later.
6.d5
Principled, but developing the g1-knight first was also sensible. 6.♘ge2 happened in Shankland-Svidler, which ended Peter's tournament after a complex game, but Vladimir chooses a different path.
6...♘e5!

The point. The knight sits extremely well on this square, thanks to the advanced h-pawn. Now f4 will always be met by ...♘eg4.

7.♗e2 h5

8.♗f4?!

In a position as complex as this one, every move is critical and the smallest nuances can have a serious impact. This feels quite normal, but since White has no better follow-up than ♘f3 anyway, he should have started with that and chosen a better place for the bishop later.

8.♘f3 is a smarter move order in any case: 8...♘xf3+ 9.gxf3 0-0, and now that the pawn structure has been clarified, it is easier to pick a good square for the c1-bishop. Placing it in front of the mobile f3-pawn looks ungainly, and ♗g5 or ♗e3 would have been clearly better. As I understand such pawn structures, the position revolves around the f4-f5 push, which White needs to time carefully. It isn't going to be easy, with Black having the ...c6 break, later followed by another one, be it ...e6 or ...f5, or perhaps by queenside expansion with ...b5. White has a strong pawn centre, but no clear shelter for his king, even in the long term.

8...0-0 9.♘f3 What else? But now the placement of the dark-squared bishop is very dubious.

9...♘xf3+ 10.gxf3 c6

It is good to get the ...c6 and ...cxd5 trade in to have an open c-file, better control over the b5-square and some room for the d8-queen to play with.

11.♕d2 cxd5 12.cxd5 ♔h7

Classy. The kingside is now just a little bit tighter, and the h6-square guarded; and if Black pushes ...f5, the soft g6-pawn is guarded, which can gain Black time.

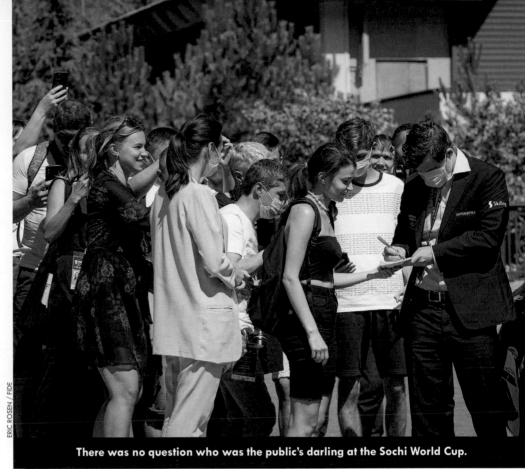

There was no question who was the public's darling at the Sochi World Cup.

13.a4?!

When you try preventing counterplay on your weaker flank, you often only delay the inevitable and weaken your position further. Black was probably going to push ...b5 at some point, but the cure is worse than the disease, and now the b3-square is weakened. Also, when ...b5 will eventually happen, Black will have more files and diagonals open for his queenside play.

13...♘d7 14.a5 White gains some space, but it is not very useful and Black can already start considering the ...b5 push, with, or even without, the preparatory ...a7-a6.

14...f5!

Magnus hits on the kingside first. The weakened g6-pawn is out of White's reach, and Black's pressure along the f-file is the primary factor here.

15.♖a3 ♘e5

The pawn push 15...b5!? would have been very timely here as well, and after the game Magnus also mentioned this motif.

16.♗e3?!

The bishop moves to a more harmonious square, where it is no longer in the way of the f3-pawn, but at the same time this allows a strong positional pawn sacrifice.

16...f4!

Black gives up the f-pawn, but gains ultimate control of the f4-square, which is crucial, since it will guarantee a solid outpost for the monster knight on e5.

17.♗xf4 ♗d7 Setting up a beautiful positional exchange sacrifice.

There was also a more laconic solution to the problem of the f4-square. 17...♖f7!? is less spectacular than what Magnus did in the game, but at least equally effective: ...♕f8 is a huge threat, and White has no better option than to give up the f4-bishop for the knight, yielding Black dark-square control at the cost of just one pawn.

18.♘d1

White guards f3 and is ready to move the f4-bishop. Obviously, Magnus had anticipated exactly this.

18...♖xf4!

Beautiful, and even though the computers assess the position as roughly equal, it was very clear that Black will be having all the fun from now on. A computer's assessment is an estimate of its own chances against itself, which doesn't always tally with how the chances between two human players are actually split.

19.♕xf4 ♗h6 20.♕g3 ♕f8!

Gaining control of the f4-square – the entire point of the sacrifice.

21.♘e3 ♗f4 22.♕g2 ♖c8
Rooks are meant for open files.

23.♖c3 Trading the potentially active c8-rook makes sense. The engine offers the bold 23.♖b3!?, estimating the position as about equal, but it is pretty scary to just ignore ...♖c1+.

23...♖xc3 24.bxc3 ♕c8

Now the queen switches to the queenside. White's pieces are in disarray, but he still has a very solid, albeit rather depressing, set-up from a defensive point of view.

25.c4 b5!?

Opening files and keeping the ...♗h3 idea, in case White castles kingside.

26.axb6 This is called en passant, noobs ☺. **26...axb6**

27.♕g1?? White basically needs to get the king to the right, so the rook can go to the left. Here he is preparing ♔f1-g2, but he is too late.

Instead, 27.♔f1 first would achieve the goal of regrouping the pieces in the right way. White can follow it up with ♔g1, ♕f1 if needed, or ♕g1, ♔g2, depending on the situation. With 27...b5 Black wins an important pawn, but White can defend if he continues with the right plan: 28.♕g1! bxc4 29.♔g2! ♕c5 30.♔a1 (White just has to make sure the h1-rook gets to participate) 30...♗xe3 31.fxe3 ♕xe3 32.♖e1, and surprisingly, White is actually alive. He has given up a bunch of pawns, but has got some coordination in return, and, with ♕c1 coming, Black's active queen will have to give up some ground.

Alternatively, 27.0-0!? would be a practical way to try and set up a defence. The rook is now ready to join the game, and if Black decides to take it, which he should, the position simplifies and the drawing tendencies increase. After 27...♗h3 28.♕h1 ♗xf1 29.♔xf1 Black can take on e3 and regain the c4-pawn as well, but that's just restoring the material balance. If Black converts his positional compensation into material, we'll probably see the game end peacefully.

27...♕a8! 28.♔f1 ♕a2!

The key, stopping the much-needed ♔g2, which would release White's queen and rook, which are still caged in. All of a sudden, White is totally paralysed.

29.♘g2 ♕a1+

This works out more than perfectly,

but objectively the cleanest win was 29...♕b1+! 30.♘e1 b5! (well-timed – computers always do that well) 31.cxb5 ♗xb5, and Black keeps White on the ropes, since 32..♗xb5? would lose to the 32...♘xf3! intermezzo. White doesn't have a move here and is just lost.

30.♘e1 ♕b2 The queen is methodically coming closer. Fedoseev had his last chance here.

31.♘g2? Playing along, but White can no longer afford this.

31.♘d3! doesn't look like much more fun – trading the only piece that might possibly attack something, but

it would still rob Black of some horse-power (pun intended): 31...♘xd3 32.♗xd3 ♕c3 33.♗e2 ♕c2 (White is almost in zugzwang) 34.♖h2! (but only almost). Without the knights, Black actually doesn't have a clear win, although to say that White is fine here would be a gross exaggeration.

31...♕c1+ 32.♘e1 ♕d2

Now White is truly stuck, since 33.♘g2 would lose to 33...♘d3!. White now has to shuffle his queen and rook, inside their cage, waiting for the finishing blow that Black inevitably will come up with.

33.♕g2 ♔g7 34.♖g1 ♔f8!?

Taking his time and moving away from any ♘d3 ♘xd3 ♕xg6+ tricks.

35.♕h1 e6! Gaining some extra squares. **36.♖g3 exd5 37.exd5 ♗f5** The bishop is better placed here, and the e5-knight is now ready to go and deal the death blow.

38.♖g1 ♔f7 39.♖g3 ♘d7 40.♖g5

40...♗xg5! In a dominant position, it is very important at some point to start cashing in. The rook can and should be picked up now.

41.hxg5 ♘e5

The threat was stronger than the execution, and White resigned. White has to move his queen and then ...♕c1 will create the deadly threat of ...♘d3. White's position is hopeless and he has been demolished and demoralized.

GRANDMASTERS GET YOUNGER AND YOUNGER

YOU'LL BE BEGGING FOR A DRAW WELL BEFORE MY AFTERNOON NAP

BEREND VONK

**NOTES BY
Peter Heine Nielsen**

**Magnus Carlsen
Vladimir Fedoseev**
Sochi World Cup 2021
(Final 3rd/4th place, Game 2)
Caro-Kann Defence, Advance Variation

1.e4 c6
Fedoseev, needing to win after his loss in the first game, does his part to ensure an unbalanced game and deviates from his usual 1...e5.
2.d4 d5 3.e5 ♗f5 4.c4!?

Typically, this is played with 4.h4 h5 included. It is unclear who benefits from excluding those moves, but it leads to less familiar structures in which the players will have to think for themselves, unable to follow well-trodden paths.
4...e6 5.♘c3 ♗b4
Here 5...♘e7 is played more often, but the game move is preferred by at least some of the computers. But, as said: we are basically in uncharted waters.
6.cxd5 ♕xd5!?

A principled move, giving Black the d5-square, where he will later place

one of his knights. As we'll see, it also means White gets access to the e4-square.
7.♘e2 ♕d8 8.a3 ♗a5 9.♘g3 ♘e7 10.♗c4 ♗g6

One could argue that Black has a pretty good Caro-Kann. The d5-square is firmly his, and ...♘d7-b6 is an easy way to utilize it. But having all the pieces on the board means Black's cramped position with one good square available is not really enough, as the other minor pieces lack obvious footholds. And Magnus immediately uses his momentum to attack:
11.h4!
Not having committed to this advance at move 4 means that White always had the option of playing it later, and Magnus, as usual, times his flank attacks well. Should Black reply with the typical ...h5, then White has the option of ♗g5, while Black, with his bishop on g6, no longer has ...♗g4 options. Interestingly, after 11...h5 the computers prefer 12.0-0, with a promising position for White.
11...h6 12.h5 ♗h7 13.♕g4

13...♔f8?!

It looked as if Fedoseev would have to give up the right to castle, as 13...♖g8 appears to be the only other way to defend the g7-pawn.
However, the interesting tactic 13...♗f5! was possible, the point being 14.♕xg7 ♖h7 trapping White's queen. 14.♘xf5 is also possible, of course, with a pleasant position for White, but nothing compared to the overwhelming advantage he has from here on in.
14.0-0 ♘d7 15.♘ce4 ♗c7 16.♗a2 ♘f5 17.♘xf5 ♗xf5 18.♕f3

Black has managed to ease the pressure a bit by exchanging a set of minor pieces, but the long-term damage to his position is irreparable. With Anand and Kramnik recently testing the 'no castle chess' version, this is a good reminder of how valuable that option is. Black's king simply has no reasonable way to long-term safety, while White's king is safely hidden away on g1.
18...♕e7 19.♘g3 ♗h7 20.♕g4 c5

21.♗d2 The immediate 21.f4 was also strong, but this is a nice little

Magnus Carlsen and Vladimir Fedoseev at the start of their second game.
It almost looks as if the Russian senses that there is another brilliancy in the air.

move, nipping any Black counter-play in the bud. If now 21...cxd4 then 22.♗b4 ♘c5 23.♖ac1 b6 24.f4 gives a crushing attack.

21...♖d8 22.f4 ♘b6 23.♗c3!

A nice move, again planning to meet 23....cxd4 with 24.♗b4!, holding back Black's counterplay.

23...♘d5 24.f5!

Magnus has restrained himself, not giving up any material yet, but that's changing now. He starts off the fire-works with an exchange sacrifice.

24...♘e3 25.♕f3 ♘xf5

25...♘xf1 was possible, but after simply 26.♖xf1, White's attack along the f-file is unstoppable. Now it comes to a temporary stop, and Magnus has to open a second front.

26.♘xf5 ♗xf5 27.d5!

Black's bishop having been lured to f5 makes this possible, since 27...exd5 is not possible because of 28.♕xf5.

27...♗b6 28.♗c4

Another move very much in the spirit of the game, limiting Black's activity

as much as possible, and avoiding ...c4+. If 28...exd5 then, for example, 29.♕xf5 dxc4 30.e6 f6 31.♗xf6 gxf6 32.♕g6 wins instantly.

28...♔g8 29.d6 ♕h4 30.b3

At first sight, Black's position may not look all that hopeless. 30...♔h7 would look like artificial castling, but the computer gives 31.a4! a5 32.g4!!, when after 32...♗xg4 33.♕e4+ ♔g8 34.♖a2 Black's position collapses due to his king being boxed in, and after 32...♕xg4+ 33.♕xg4 ♗xg4 34.♖xf7 the inclusion of a4/...a5 means that ♖xb7 will threaten the now unpro-tected bishop at b6.

30...♖d7 31.♕e2 ♕g4

Fedoseev had a fantastic World Cup, and the games in this mini-match do not change that impression, despite him being on the wrong side of two brilliancies. It takes two to create a good game, and Fedoseev does his best to fight, forcing Magnus to take extraordinary measures – and the World Champion certainly obliges:

32.♖xf5!! ♕xf5 Black could get an endgame with 32...♕xe2, but after 33.♗xe2 exf5 34.♗b5!? ♖d8 35.♗c4 Black's situation is tragic, despite him being an exchange and a pawn up. There is no way he'll manage to free himself, and 36.♖f1 will be next, when his position collapses.

33.♖f1 ♕g5 34.♗d2 ♕d8 35.♕g4

35...a6 Easy to criticize, but Black practically is in zugzwang. This prepares ...♕e8 without allowing ♗b5. But obviously, Magnus strikes before Black manages to consolidate. 35...♔h7 would not change anything, as 36.♖xf7 ♖xf7 37.♕g6+ ♔g8 38.♕xe6 leads to a similar kind of position.

36.♖xf7!! The f7-pawn was the foundation of Black's position. Now 36...♖xf7 37.♕xe6 ♕f8 38.♕g6 leaves Black completely boxed in.

36...♔xf7

Magnus's double rook sacrifice wins by pure strength of position, and no calculations are basically necessary!

It is striking how helpless Black is, despite actually being two rooks up for a bishop. But the remaining white pieces and pawns coordinate so well that a normal material count has absolutely no relevance.

37.♕xe6+!?

The human touch. The computer gives 37.♗xe6+ ♔e8 38.♕g6+ ♔f8 39.♗xd7 ♕xd7 40.e6, winning, but the interesting part of Magnus's double rook sacrifice is that it wins by pure strength of position, and that no calculations are basically necessary!

37...♔f8 38.♕f5+ ♔e8 39.♕g6+ ♔f8 40.♕f5+ ♔e8 41.♕g6+ ♔f8 42.e6!

42...♕f6

Also the computer's preferred move. After 42...♖e7 it gives 43.♕f5+ ♔e8 44.♗f4!, protecting d6, when Black is completely stuck for a reasonable move.

43.exd7! ♕xg6 44.hxg6

If Black thinks that the pressure has been lifted, he is hallucinating. He is still completely boxed in, and if 44...h5 then 45.♗g5! with mate!

44...♗d8 45.♗e6 h5 46.♔f2 h4 47.♗g4!

Staying loyal to the theme of the game till the end. ...♖h5 will not be allowed, so Black remains unable to stir.

47...b5 48.♔f3 b4

Here 48...♖h6 might look as the only way to fight, but the opposite-coloured bishop ending after 49.♗xh6 gxh6 is easily winning, as the white king can walk to c8 unchallenged, and White's bishop on f5 is covering the g6-pawn as well as preventing a possible black pawn from queening.

49.axb4 cxb4

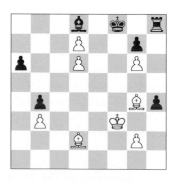

But at the same time, as he made his move, Vladimir Fedoseev resigned. ∎

‹O› Meltwater
CHAMPIONS CHESS TOUR
2021

The Finals

25TH SEPTEMBER – 4TH OCTOBER

KO is OK for Kosteniuk

Former World Champion prevails in Women's World Cup

ANASTASIIAKOROLKOVA

The Women's World Cup saw an all-Russian final between Alexandra Kosteniuk and Alexandra Goryachkina. Not for the first time, Kosteniuk showed her expertise in knock-out competitions and took the title. **VLADIMIR BARSKY** asked the winner why the format appeals to her.

I t is difficult to say if it is a good idea to hold the Women's World Cup in parallel with the men's or if it's better to hold it as a separate event. This time FIDE had little choice and decided to stage the two together, which obviously had its pros and cons. Inevitably, the main attention of the fans was focused on the tournament in which Magnus Carlsen was playing. On the other hand, the Women's Cup was well worth watching and almost all the strongest players took part, with the exception of World Champion Ju Wenjun, the leader of the rating list Hou Yifan, and India's number one Humpy Koneru.

Women's chess is entertaining, emotional, and has its own stable audience. As for the sports side, there were far fewer surprises than in the men's competition (or Open section, we should say). Already in the 1/8 finals, only the well-known favourites were still in contention, all players who have been in the elite for several years. And the winner was Alexandra Kosteniuk, who always plays exceptionally well in knockout tournaments. At the closing ceremony we asked her to share her thoughts on her affinity for the knockout format.

'It would have been hard to predict that I would win this World Cup.

I managed to enter the tournament with a good mind-set: just playing chess – move after move, game after game. This sounds easier than it is, trust me. Amazingly, it's almost twenty years ago that I reached my first knockout final in the Women's World Championship in Moscow in 2001. That tournament was similar to this one in that no one, including myself, really expected to see me in the final. In Moscow, I was 17 years old, and it was my first World Championship, my first experience at such high level. Yet I reached the final, narrowly losing to Zhu Chen on tie-break.

'Another knockout highlight was definitely my victory in the Women's World Championship tournament of 2008 in Nalchik, where I went on to win the title. If we compare that victory with my win here, the similarity is that I didn't require any tie-break games throughout the event – something that's equally hard to believe as seeing myself winning these two events.

'I don't know, maybe the format just suits me. Here you need to focus on a match of two or four games, play in short segments. Longer competitions are more difficult for me, when I have to focus for two weeks of struggle. If something starts to go wrong there, it's very difficult. And here, if you lose, you finish the tournament and go home! From my perspective it is easier to focus for shorter periods. Especially for older chess players, to whom I now, oddly enough, belong at 37, this format works well. Each victory in a match is like a victory in a tournament, it gives you extra energy.

'It's hard to say which was my toughest match. The matches with Maria Muzychuk, Valentina Gunina and Alexandra Goryachkina all followed the same scenario: in the first game, regardless of the colour of the pieces, I got a position in the range from "dangerous" to "lost", and then somehow I miraculously either escaped, or even won. Of

'The format works well for me. Each victory in a mini-match is like a victory in a tournament, it gives you extra energy'

course, if the matches are so short, such a victory completely changes the logic of the struggle. After all, your opponent cannot just play chess when a draw in the next game is tantamount to defeat. On the other hand, the positions were very difficult, and mistakes do not appear out of the blue. I'm glad I was lucky this time! And if I have to choose one game as my best effort, I go for the win against Maria Muzychuk.'

NOTES BY
Alexandra Kosteniuk

Maria Muzychuk
Alexandra Kosteniuk
Sochi World Cup 2021 (4.2)
Italian Game, Giuoco Piano

The following game, the second game of my 1/8 final match against Maria Muzychuk, was awarded a 'platinum crown' by one of the sponsors of the event, Nornickel, as the best game of Round 4. After a hard-fought draw as White in the first game, I now played with the black pieces.
1.e4 e5 2.♘f3 ♘c6 3.♗c4 ♗c5 4.c3 ♘f6 5.d3 0-0 6.0-0 d5!?

There are many good set-ups for Black against the 'Giuoco Piano', but the system with the immediate ...d5 is

the most direct approach against the Italian Game.
7.exd5 ♘xd5
Every move right now is a cross-roads, there being so many move orders and nuances in this system. To play or not to play a4, to include or to postpone the move h3 – these are just a few questions that I'd love to know the correct responses to. The system with ...d5 has seen many high-level games, and even top GMs sometimes got lost in all these move orders. I recall the game between Sergey Karjakin and Levon Aronian in Wijk aan Zee 2017, in which Black misplayed this line and could have lost a piece as early as on move 11.

8.♖e1
Look at another opening catastrophe that happened at top-level: 8.a4 a6 9.♖e1 ♗g4 10.♘bd2 ♔h8? 11.h3 ♗h5 12.♘e4 ♗a7 13.♘g3 ♗g6 14.♘xe5, and Duda won against So in 25 moves in the Moscow Grand Prix 2019.
8...♗g4 9.h3 ♗h5 10.♘bd2 ♘b6 11.♗b3
One of the many moves that have been played here by White, but lately ♗b3 seems to have become quite trendy. White moves the bishop to a safer square and is getting ready to play ♘e4. The only problem is that after ♗b3 the d3-pawn is left unprotected.

11...♚h8

Here, 11...♛xd3 would be the most critical reply, of course: 12.♘xe5 ♛f5 (12...♝xd1?! won't equalize, as has been borne out in several games. And 12...♛g3 is tempting, but doesn't quite work for Black either: 13.♛xh5 ♛xf2+ 14.♚h2 ♛xe1 15.♘df3, and Black is suffering) 13.♘ef3. Many games have been played with this, and the ensuing positions are quite complex. In the game, I didn't feel ready to enter all these discussions and decided to take refuge in one of the sub-lines.

12.♘e4 ♝d6

Levon Aronian has tried two other moves here that deserve attention: 12...♝e7 and 12...♘d7.

13.g4 Here, after 13.♘g3, I can simply move to g6, since the pawn on e5 is protected now.

13...♝g6

14.♘g3

This knight move prepares a kingside pawn march that we will discuss a bit later, but the central breakthrough d4 seems to be much stronger.
After 14.d4!? exd4 15.♘xd4, 15...♜e8!? sets up a deadly (well, I tend to exaggerate) trap. 16.♘xc6 bxc6

ANALYSIS DIAGRAM

17.♘xd6 (17.♝c2?? was the trap I was talking about: 17...♝xe4 18.♝xe4 ♜xe4 19.♜xe4 ♝h2+) 17...♜xe1+ 18.♛xe1 cxd6, when White has the two bishops but a weakened king position, which gives Black counter-chances.

14...♘d7 15.♝c2 a5 16.h4 h6

The key moment of the game. White opted for a very double-edged plan, which included a pawn march on the

Sochi World Cup 2021	
7 rounds of knock-out	
Quarter Finals	
Goryachkina-Saduakassova	1½-½
A.Muzychuk-Dzagnidze	3-1
Kosteniuk-Gunina	2-0
Tan Zhongyi-Lagno	1½-½
Semi-Finals	
Goryachkina-A.Muzychuk	1½-½
Kosteniuk-Tan Zhongyi	1½-½
Final 3rd/4th place	
Tan Zhongyi-A.Muzychuk	2½-1½
Final 1st/2nd place	
Kosteniuk-Goryachkina	1½-½

kingside. We've all heard that pawns cannot move backwards, and with every advance of the h- and g-pawns White's king's position looks more vulnerable. With this risky plan the stakes are high – one wrong move and the position could collapse.

17.h5?!

It was still possible to hold the balance with 17.g5!? f5 (I would probably have opted for this move in the game. Although 17...h5 is possible, I doubt I would have played it, because it means sacrificing this pawn after 18.♘h2, and even though Black does get compensation, it doesn't look so obvious to the human eye: 18...f5!? 19.♘xh5 ♘c5.) 18.gxh6

ANALYSIS DIAGRAM

and now the real chaos breaks loose. Many moves are possible, including ...f4, ...♘f6 and ...♜g8, but compared to the game White's position is not hopeless.

17...♝h7 18.g5 This was the last moment to stop (with 18.♝d2 or 18.♚g2), but White decides to go all-in.

18...f5! Not a hard move to make, but sometimes even obvious moves can be very strong.

19.gxh6? The last step into the abyss. It was time to strike in the centre with 19.d4!? when, even though the position is already quite dubious for White, Black would need to solve much harder problems than in the game, e.g. 19...exd4 (after 19...f4 20.♗xh7 fxg3 21.♗b1 gxf2+ 22.♔xf2 exd4 23.♕d3 it's almost mate on h7, but there is 23...♖xf3+! 24.♕xf3 ♘ce5... Can you assess this position?) 20.cxd4 f4 21.♘e4, and despite the computer assessing the position as favouring Black, to me the position looks completely unclear.
19...gxh6 20.♗xh6 ♖g8 21.♗b3

21...♕f6 The strongest move, but pushing the f-pawn was also quite good: 21...f4 22.♗xg8 ♕xg8 23.♘g5. During the game I didn't like this position, because I only calculated 23...fxg3 24.♕f3, after which things seemed quite unclear to me. But Black in fact has the deadly 23...♗f8!, and should be winning.
22.♗xg8 ♖xg8 23.♘g5 ♖xg5 24.♘xg5 ♕xg5

Quite a position! White has two rooks for three minor pieces but her king's position is quite weak and there are

no open files to use the rooks. White's position is simply hopeless.
25.♔f1 ♘f6 Moving my pieces closer to the white king, improving my position little by little. White can only sit and watch everything falling apart. **26.♕f3 ♘g4 27.♕g2 e4**

Opening up the h2-b8 diagonal so that square h2 will be covered after ...f4-f3, and I have the ...♘h2 idea.
28.d4 Or 28.dxe4 f4 29.♘f5 f3, with ...♘h2+ on the next move, winning.
28...♘d8! Heading to f4! During the game I also calculated some straight-forward lines, e.g. 28...♘xf2, but this just didn't feel right – there is no need to hurry.
29.c4 In case White tries to stop the knight's journey to f4 with 29.d5, it will go to e5 via f7 and then on to f3 or d3.
29...♘e6 30.c5 ♗f8 31.♖ad1 ♘f4 32.♕h1 ♗g8

And now it's time for the bishop to get to the centre.
33.♘xe4 33.b3 ♗d5 will just force White to resign; a very sad position for White. **33...♗c4+ 34.♔g1 fxe4** White resigned. A nice game to win and a tournament to remember ☺. ∎

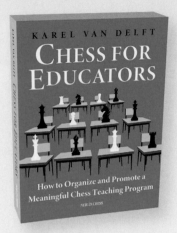

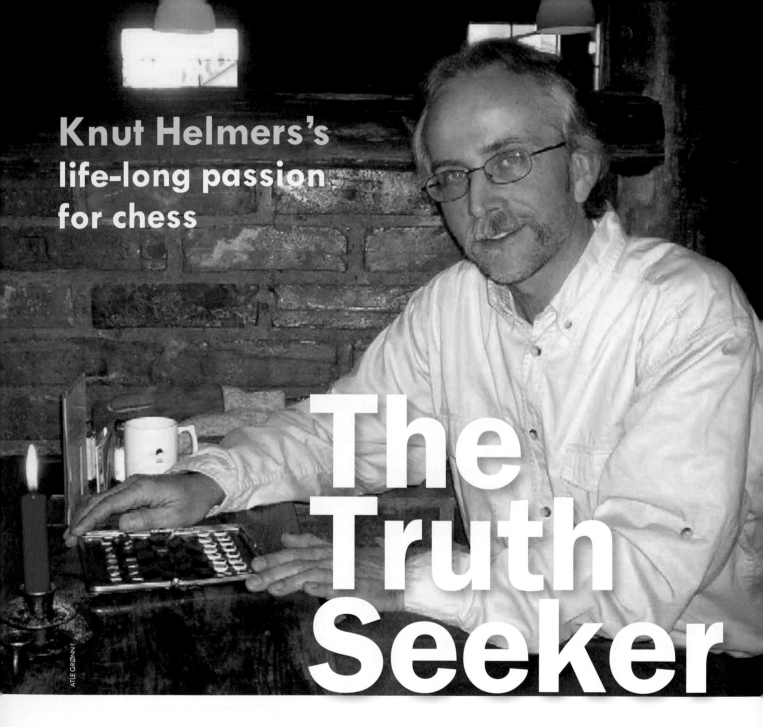

The Truth Seeker

ATLE GRØNN

He sought the truth in every position. He devoted his whole life to chess, and loved the game like few others. By mostly keeping to himself in his large den, Knut Jøran Helmers (1957-2021) shaped his own mythical status in the Norwegian chess community. **ATLE GRØNN** portrays the man who will be remembered as 'the coach of the coach of the World Champion', the man who polished the raw chess talent of Simen Agdestein in the 1980s.

Garry Kasparov was right when, in 2005, he called Norway 'the backyard of chess', although there were a few bright spots. From 1970 until his death in 1996, Arnold J. Eikrem organized a total of 187 tournaments at Gausdal Høyfjellshotell, a three-to-four-hour drive from Oslo. It was in Gausdal, in the hotel lobby in the mountains, that Knut Jøran Helmers developed the concept 'shake and throw', borrowed from the innocuous board game Ludo. Just roll the die and see what will happen. Many years later, Simen Agdestein passed this way of thinking on to Magnus

not in his basement analysing chess, he spent his time climbing Norwegian mountain peaks above 2,000 meters, finding shelter for the night in a simple tent. With the exception of an interview he granted me in December 2003 for *Norsk Sjakkblad*, he never spoke publicly. He never commented on the surreal successes of Magnus Carlsen, who lived and worked in the same city.

The myth took form: Helmers was the professional chess player who did not play chess (he quit in April 1986), who did not write about chess (his last words in print appeared in April 1991), and who stopped having

Walks at Gausdal

Helmers's name will forever be linked to Simen Agdestein's. The two very different personalities complemented each other perfectly at the chess board. Shortly after their collaboration started in 1985, 17-year-old Agdestein became the youngest grandmaster in the world.

Helmers was stubborn. He had his own principles and habits, which the people around didn't always find easy to accept. In the summer of 1981, the 24-year-old Helmers had first met the 14-year-old Agdestein, when the former organized a training session for junior players prior to the Norwegian championship. Simen had received a special invitation to participate in the top section, the elite group in the national championship, despite his modest national rating of 2164. Helmers firmly opposed this idea: Simen should play with the other youngsters.

Simen rejected his advice and made his debut in the national elite, where Helmers was the big favourite. In their encounter, Helmers had to settle for a draw. The level of chess in

Helmers became more and more reclusive, keeping the chess community at a distance for the last 30 years of his life

Carlsen. Just keep the game going, sooner or later you will be rewarded for your patience.

Helmers himself could not patiently 'shake and throw' at the chessboard. Although a chess professional, he was terrified of professional chess. He found shelter in analytical studies and remained virtually unknown outside Scandinavia. But the few of us who met him realized that the man with the moustache and the rolling tobacco (the classic Norwegian brand Petterøe's No. 3) represented a rare and unparalleled scientific approach to the game.

He played through all games in *Chess Informants* 1-40 by hand, with a physical board and pieces, long before the computer mouse became part of every chess player's tool kit. Anyone who has opened an old *Chess Informant* from Belgrade on the opening code A00 with the goal of reaching E99, knows how slowly the hand works.

Over the years, Helmers became more and more reclusive, keeping the chess community at a distance for the last 30 years of his life. When he was

students (his last known student was Jon Ludvig Hammer in 2005). Nevertheless, he remained a 'professional' chess lover until he died at the age of 64 on April 21, 2021.

Knut Helmers (Board 2) keeps a close watch on Simen Agdestein (Board 1) as the young star is on his way to a grandmaster norm at the 1984 Thessaloniki Olympiad.

ØYSTEIN BREKKE

Norway being low, Simen finished in 4th place, while Helmers shared first place. Helmers later withdrew from the play-off after a public argument with the Federation about the playing venue. Shortly after the Norwegian championship, Helmers became Nordic champion in Reykjavik.

One of his clients at the time was the Finnish grandmaster Yrjö Rantanen.

More than chess lessons only. Simen Agdestein highly enjoyed the talks during his walks with Knut Helmers, intellectual adventures that introduced him to a new world.

Helmers-Rantanen
Reykjavik 1981
position after 14...♕b4

15.♘db5 cxb5 16.♘xb5 1-0.

In the early 1980s, Helmers was capable of beating some famous players, for example the Yugoslav grandmaster Predrag Nikolic.

Helmers-Nikolic
Esbjerg 1982
position after 35...♖e7

36.♖xf7 ♕d7 36...♖xf7 37.♕e8+ ♔c7 38.♕c8 mate. **37.♖f8+ ♔c7 38.♕c4+** 1-0.

It was more typical for him, however, to go for a draw. His respect for Eastern European masters – whom he had studied in detail – was out of proportion. His early draw offers were often, though not always, turned down. At the 1980 Chess Olympiad in Malta, defending the first board for Norway, Helmers managed to draw against his hero, the Romanian grandmaster Florin Gheorghiu. In 2003 Helmers told me: '[Norwegian chess legend] Svein Johannessen had two pictures hanging over his bed: his mother-in-law on one side, and Keres on the other. I would rather choose Gheorghiu. He was phenomenal with the white pieces.'

At the Olympiad in Lucerne in 1982, Helmers was again Norway's number one, now with Simen Agdestein at the fourth board. Simen won the gold medal on his board, but Helmers was still critical of the 15-year-old boy's game. In *Norsk Sjakkblad* 1983/2, Helmers wrote: 'Simen's greatest weakness is probably in tactics, and it would be wise of him to adjust his opening repertoire accordingly.' The article ends with Helmers's clean victory against Simen's Petroff Defence from a Gausdal tournament.

However, in the next issue, 1983/3, Helmers praised Simen's game for the first time: 'Simen has a good eye for transitional phases, and his technique is amazingly good.' Helmers was always honest in his evaluations.

What Simen himself remembers best from this period and all the Gausdal tournaments is not the chess content, but the walks with Helmers in the Norwegian mountains. 'It was the same walk every day. It took maybe an hour, and for me it was an adventure to take part in conversations with the "adult world". This was something quite different from school back home.'

Spassky

Grandmaster Genna Sosonko remembers a tournament in the Nordic chess capital, Reykjavik, in 1980. At the time, Sosonko lived in the Helmersstraat in Amsterdam, named after an 18th-century Dutch author.

'Seeing the name of the Norwegian master Helmers among the participants, I even asked myself – why should that be? But I did not get particularly worried: A Norwegian? A chess player? A quarter of a century would still have to pass before a gigantic oak would cast its shadow over the stunted grass of the Norwegian chess lawn.' (translated from a Russian article on chess-news.ru, 2020)

Helmers offered a draw, but Sosonko declined and responded with a winning combination.

In the summer of 1983, it was time for Norwegian chess to step up a level when some of the best foreigners announced their arrival. It was easy to pick out three Norwegians for the super-tournament, a round-robin in the small town of Gjøvik, organized by tireless chess promoter Øystein Brekke. It had to be our two top players, IM Leif Øgaard (born 1951), IM Helmers, and Agdestein as the joker.

The three Norwegians had the lowest ratings in the field. Norway was still the little brother in Scandinavia, without a single grandmaster; no Ulf Andersson (Sweden), no Bent Larsen (Denmark), no Fridrik Olafsson (Iceland).

Simen was barely 16 years old, naive and fearless. He beat Boris Spassky in a chaotic game and made a plus score. Helmers knew everything about their intimidating opponents, and referred to Tony Miles as 'The Butcher'. 'How can one fight on equal terms with such an attitude?' Simen wondered.

The Norwegian clash in Round 6 showed that Helmers completely lacked self-confidence when he resigned in an inferior, but materially equal position.

Helmers-Agdestein
Gjøvik 1983
final position, after 36...e5 (0-1)

'Helmers was clearly uncomfortable facing a teenager who had reached the level of the best Norwegian players without years of training,' Agdestein says today.

In the next round, a heated discussion broke out in the analysis room when Helmers resigned after 25 moves against John Nunn, in a position in which several amateurs in the audience thought that the local hero had the upper hand. Modern computer evaluations favour Nunn's position, but at the time it was far from clear.

Nunn-Helmers
Gjøvik 1983
final position, after 25.♖f1 (1-0)

Spassky was the big name in Gjøvik, but not an obvious favourite. He played seven dry draws. After the game, he lit a cigarette and strolled to the tennis court. By winning the last round against Helmers, Spassky saved his reputation and a 50% score. Helmers did not believe the ex-champion would give him a draw and chose to play over-aggressively as Black. 'Why don't you just play normal chess?' Simen had suggested the day before the game.

Karpov

1984 was not a good chess year for Helmers. The reigning world champion Anatoly Karpov came to Oslo for a tournament that was even stronger than that in Gjøvik the year before. Øgaard and Helmers considered themselves professionals and refused to play for free 'like pure amateurs' on their home turf. In the end, Agdestein was the only Norwegian in the field. Karpov won, while

Passing on wisdom

Knut Helmers (1957-2021) never worked with Magnus Carlsen, but there is a distinct line that connects the two. As a coach and thinker, Helmers had a big influence on Simen Agdestein (1967), who became the youngest grandmaster in the world (at the time) at the age of 17 and was Norway's strongest chess player for many years.

Simen Agdestein, in his turn, was the first real coach of Magnus Carlsen (1990). He was at Carlsen's side at numerous events, providing useful advice and insights, even if he was always the first to belittle his contribution given his pupil's phenomenal talent. In 2004 Agdestein wrote *Wonderboy, How Magnus Carlsen Became the Youngest Chess Grandmaster in the World* (which then was 13 years).

Perhaps some of the lessons **Magnus Carlsen** learned from Agdestein were seen when he acted as an inspiring and supportive first board of the young Norwegian Olympiad team. Whether the World Champion will one day coach a next Norwegian talent, only the future can tell. (DJtG)

Simen put in another good performance and beat world-class grandmaster Vlastimil Hort, as well as some other players.

Helmers was nevertheless overtly critical when Agdestein was given first board for Norway in the Chess Olympiad in Thessaloniki later that year – ahead of the more experienced Helmers and Øgaard. However, the teenager convincingly scored his first GM norm (beating Hort again) and was now clearly Norway's strongest player.

In the meantime, Leif Øgaard had given up his professional career and the hunt for the GM title. Helmers, our only remaining chess pro, struggled more and more with his nerves and could hardly sleep during tournaments. He preferred to play as little as possible. When Agdestein caught a cold in Thessaloniki, Helmers accused the teenager of pretending to be sick to avoid playing chess. Simen just shook his head in bewilderment – he would rather play every single round.

Fortunately, after the Olympiad, the small Norwegian chess family managed to team up Helmers with Agdestein. 'I am eternally grateful for what Helmers did for me in the mid 80s. Helmers lacked fighting instincts, while I had big knowledge gaps, so we were a perfect match. Helmers also taught me to avoid time-trouble, a serious weakness of mine. I used to invent the wheel in each game, which cost time. With Helmers on my team, everything went smoothly,' Simen remembers.

Time to quit

Around this time, the American IM Jonathan Tisdall (born 1958) settled in Norway, first via Eikrem's Gausdal tournaments and later via a Norwegian chess-playing girlfriend, Marianne Hagen. Tisdall invited Helmers to join forces to help each other towards the GM title.

In a closed GM tournament at Easter 1986 in Oslo, Helmers lost to Tisdall, the rude newcomer who declined his draw offer. Tisdall combined nicely and checkmated Helmers on move 27. The following

Simen Agdestein: 'Helmers lacked fighting instincts, while I had big knowledge gaps, so we were a perfect match'

Jonathan Tisdall (left) playing against Einar Gausel (who would become a GM in 1995) in a team match in Oslo in 1986.

week, at Gausdal, they met again in what was to be Helmers's last tournament.

Helmers-Tisdall
Gausdal 1986
position after 25...♗xa3

26.♕c3 26.bxa3 ♖b8+; 26.♗e4 ♕a5. **26...♗xb2 27.♔xb2 f5 28.♕f6+ ♔c8 29.♕c3+ ♔d8 30.♕f6+ ♔c8 31.♕f8+ ♔c7 32.♖c1+ ♔b6 33.♕b4+** 1-0.

Helmers got his revenge. 'You should play in this style against the others as well,' Tisdall said, 'then you will become a GM.' Helmers responded by quitting competitive chess. He also ended all communication with his rival Tisdall.

Rerouting the c8-bishop

Chess was so important to Helmers that he could no longer play. For the next 35 years, he was a pure chess analyst. His greatest success as a trainer came early, in 1986, when 19-year-old Agdestein won the Lloyds Bank tournament with a score of 8 out of 9. In London, Agdestein revealed what the duo had been working on for some time: the Dutch Stonewall, with a completely new dynamic concept of the 'bad bishop' on c8.

Murey/Van der Sterren-Agdestein
London 1986
(both 0-1)

The Stonewall is heavy and static. The black pawns in the centre are blocked on ice-cold light squares. Until the mid-1980s, Black's light-squared bishop was stuck behind the wall or forced to embark on the long march c8-d7-e8-h5. Then, a new route was discovered for the bishop to b7 (pointing towards g2) or a6 (pointing towards f1).

In his debut at Lloyds Bank, Agdestein won two strategic masterpieces with the Stonewall. Many triumphs were to follow with this new Norwegian weapon. The ideas of Helmers and Agdestein from the 1980s firmly stood the test of time, as demonstrated by Magnus Carlsen in 2015 with black victories against Anand and Caruana.

The right file for the rook

In Nordic chess, Helmers gained a reputation as a great theorist. The Swede Harry Schüssler took the trip to Oslo to learn from the perfectionist. Helmers set the goal of finding *the truth* about the optimal placement of the rooks, the answer to the perennial question: which rook should move to d1?

Helmers later told me: 'Schüssler and I looked at the Tartakower Variation of the Queen's Gambit for a week before we could address this issue. Today players go, say, ♖ad1, without thinking. If it turns out that the rook belongs on c1, you can always play ♖c1 later. I dislike that kind of correction. Chess is very concrete, which should encourage a quest for the truth. Unfortunately, chess reflects society in general; players no longer have the time to immerse themselves

in the position and find the optimal placement for the rooks.'

Schüssler returned to Sweden and became a GM shortly afterwards. Helmers remained intrigued by how difficult it is to find the absolute truth in chess all his life. Consequently, he refused to use exclamation marks, question marks or other subjective markers in his publications.

Helmers wrote a long weekly chess column in the Norwegian newspaper *Arbeiderbladet*, in which he analysed international top chess. Only a handful of readers could understand the depth of his insights, but Helmers refused to vulgarize his chess language.

Nevertheless, he admitted in 2003 that the use of exclamation marks can be a powerful stylistic tool: 'Gheorghiu was full of passion. His exclamation marks reflected his physical way of playing. The harder he slammed the piece onto its destination square, the more exclamation marks he would use.'

Lessons in science

My first training sessions with Helmers around 1986-87 made a deep impression. Helmers was intelligent, funny, and sarcastic. I immediately liked him, dazzled by his chess knowledge. During one of our first meetings, I was supposed to show one of my own games. I modestly chose a game I had lost as Black against an Austrian junior.

I knew White's standard plan in the Réti Opening with c4, b3, etc. Here I told Helmers that my opponent had

found a new idea. 'What could that be?' Helmers asked. '♕e1 followed by e4 and ♕e2', I said with naive enthusiasm. Helmers smiled mischievously before he ridiculed me with some well-placed sarcasm. The set-up was well-known among the experts. I had not done my homework properly.

This was a useful lesson. I learned to respect established knowledge. The next time we met, I made sure to raise my level and not produce any nonsense.

I loved the training sessions with Helmers. It was very motivating that I could actually understand what he was talking about. He had a national training programme for a group of very young talents who all quit chess after working with the guru. Helmers enjoyed working with me. Still, even though we lived in the same city and he was well paid for our sessions, it was always difficult to arrange specific meetings.

A few years later, we met again. I showed him a draw I made against a Czech IM. Helmers's face lit up. 'The Czech school, including Hort, Smejkal and Jansa, was fantastic', Helmers sighed.

We dug into the Catalan. The first fundamental decision concerned the bishop on c1. Should we go for ♗d2, ♗f4 or ♗g5 ?

Helmers was strongly influenced by one of the most boring games in the history of chess, Kasparov-Karpov, 20th game 1986, in which the bishop went to g5. He was convinced that Kasparov knew what he was doing. As he wrote in his chess column a few years later, on July 14, 1990: 'It is no wonder that Soviet chess players are still at the forefront of launching important novelties. There, unlike in Norway, the ideas are not left to arrogant dilettantes, but are analysed by knowledgeable people.'

10.♗g5 ♘bd7 11.♗xf6 ♘xf6 12.♘bd2 ♖c8 13.♘b3 c5 14.dxc5 ♗d5 15.♖fd1 ♗xb3 16.♕xb3 ♕c7 17.a4 ♕xc5 18.axb5 axb5

19.♘d4 b4 20.e3 ♖fd8 21.♖d2 ♕b6

½-½ (Kasparov-Karpov, 20th match game 1986).

Helmers thought the improvement was hidden in the last diagram. White plays 19.♖a5 instead, with the idea of 19...♖b8 20.♘d4, and the weaknesses on b5 and c6 become evident. Helmers showed me his subtle analyses. Already in 1986, a couple of months after the WC match, Helmers wrote a dry book in Norwegian about the games from the third K-K match, in which he analysed 19.♖a5.

The move 10.♗g5 (with the idea of 19.♖a5) became part of my own repertoire for many years. I never had the chance to use 19.♖a5 in practical play, but I learned a lot about the scientific method in chess before the computer area.

Money and chess

There is no doubt that Helmers loved the game like almost no one else I have met. Since he could not play himself, it became all the more important for him to realize his dreams through Agdestein. He wrote a beautiful little book in Norwe-

gian in 1987, in which he provided in-depth comments to 12 games by Simen Agdestein.

Agdestein, on the other hand, no longer had the time or motivation to work with Helmers. He participated in elite tournaments with Kasparov in Tilburg and Belgrade in 1989, but his daily focus was mostly on football and university studies.

Agdestein quickly became a well-known public figure in Norway and in 1988 was the first and only chess player to receive a yearly salary from the state of approximately 10,000 dollars. A year later, the young and talented grandmaster received fierce criticism from the editor of *Norsk Sjakkblad* for bringing chess into disrepute by not investing himself fully in the board game. In the same issue of *Norsk Sjakkblad*, a well-known Norwegian chess journalist, Thor Støre, even claimed that Agdestein's football commitment was the biggest scandal in Norwegian chess history since our participation in the Nazi Olympiad in 1936.

In hindsight, the attacks on Agdestein look bizarre (as they also did back then). However, on several occasions, Helmers backed up the 'attackers'. In his chess column on July 15, 1989, Helmers wholeheartedly supported the harsh line of *Norsk Sjakkblad* against Agdestein, and on June 16, 1990, Helmers demanded that the Federation award the highest honour (a badge in 'gold') to chess journalist Støre, who was the most rabid critic of Agdestein's football career.

Helmers followed up with several critical chess columns about his former student Agdestein who, meanwhile, had been selected for the Norwegian national football team. 'It borders on immorality if the state scholarship is used for playing football,' Helmers wrote on March 16, 1991, in a long article entitled 'Money and chess'. Shortly afterwards, his chess column in *Arbeiderbladet* was cancelled.

When I ask Simen today about the controversy, he barely remembers it. He doesn't recall reading the criticism from the small chess community – he was far too busy with football at the time. In that sense, he justifies his critics somewhat. In 1991, Agdestein was at the height of his career (soon everything fell apart – both football and chess; but that is another story).

Helmers could never accept that Agdestein did not fully explore his chess talent. In Agdestein, Helmers had found someone who could accomplish what he himself had dreamt of, but then Simen wanted to control his own life. Helmers never got over this 'betrayal'.

Agdestein didn't take Helmers's reaction to heart and was happy to work with him again for a match against the new British star, Michael Adams, in Oslo in 1994. At the time, Agdestein was injured, depressed, and was giving up both football and chess. Helmers came in handy. The match ended 2-2. The renewed collaboration gave Agdestein a new weapon: Alekhine's Defence with an early exchange on e5 and development of the bishop to g7.

Adams-Agdestein
Oslo 1994 (4th match game)
position after 4.♘f3

4...dxe5 5.♘xe5 g6 6.♗c4 c6
(0-1, 35 moves)
As for the Stonewall, the Alekhine has also been passed on from Agdestein to Carlsen.

At the beginning of the 2000s, Agdestein offered Helmers a permanent coaching job at the elite sport school outside Oslo, but Helmers said no.

The last interview

For the next 10 years, after the Agdestein-Adams match, there was no news from Helmers. I had a research career at the university, but my interest in chess was still there, so I agreed to become editor of *Norsk Sjakkblad* purely as a hobby from December 2003. The first thing I did was to call Helmers at his home (he didn't have a mobile phone – and would only get one 15 years later).

He surprised me by accepting my invitation to an interview. He lived in the same big house in a nice area of Oslo, with his own floor (the basement) filled with chess. He had a wife, whom I never met, and two kids, who were never taught to play chess.

'Chess has become a sport,' he complained even before the Carlsen era had begun. Helmers expressed his admiration for the old school: 'Geller's sense of dynamism was incredible. He could make the worst Tartakower bishop on c8 spit fire. Alas, the likes of Geller, Polugaevsky and Balashov (Karpov's second) could not become World Champions. They were idealists, truth-seekers.'

Helmers emphasized that chess is logical: 'Your position cannot be bad after only good moves. This is the basis for a scientific approach to chess.'

How did he view the development of modern chess theory? 'Nothing much has happened since the Hedgehog in the 70s. The game is more uncompromising today, but theoretically we are still at an early stage of development. Admittedly, much is known about static factors, but how should one assess, say, whether space advantage can compensate for a bad bishop?'

Helmers told me that he worked continuously on chess and did not rule out the possibility of a comeback as a player. Still, when I left him that

Leif Øgaard (left) and Knut Helmers analyse their game at the Oslo Easter tournament in 1986. On the right the Norwegian player Odd Flater (1919-89), who was a friend of Helmers.

night, I understood that the mythical truth-seeker would never again sit at the table with a physical opponent.

Bad bishop, strong pawn

A few enthusiasts in the Norwegian chess community, including Leif Øgaard, hoped that Helmers could be a trainer for Magnus, who was regularly punished in the opening by the

Helmers emphasized that chess is logical: 'Your position cannot be bad after only good moves'

world elite in and around 2005. This was not to be, but Helmers at least had some sessions with 15-year-old Jon Ludvig Hammer.

Hammer says that Helmers decided that they should work on static and dynamic pawn structures in Euwe's books on the middlegame. When he comments on Norwegian TV today, Hammer from time to time quotes Helmers's characteristic aphorisms. An example is Helmers's evaluation

of Sicilian structures with a bishop on e7 and a pawn on d6: 'A bad bishop protects a good pawn'.

In his final years, Helmers only had contact with Leif Øgaard (who surprisingly earned the GM title in 2007, 25 years after his retirement from professional chess). Øgaard says that they regularly discussed chess theory, despite Helmers suffering from brain cancer the last two years. Two weeks before his death, they analysed the Catalan and the Rubinstein Variation of the French. Interestingly enough, Helmers never acquired modern tools like ChessBase. He had a computer, but preferred to work with handwritten notes, as he had always done.

Helmers's son confirmed to me the day before the funeral that his father was constantly smoking his 'rolleys' and writing down mysterious chess notes. He never talked about chess with his family, but he always asked his son to buy him rolling tobacco. ∎

Atle Grønn (b. 1971), Norwegian chess commentator and chess writer, international master, professor of Russian linguistics. He is currently writing a book about Simen Agdestein.

Magnus Carlsen teaches chess

A beautiful sacrifice that remained hidden

Magnus Carlsen shares a dear memory from the 2004 Dubai Open, the tournament where as a 13-year-old he scored his third and final grandmaster norm.

Carlsen-Vladimirov
Dubai Open 2004
position after 21.♕e4

This position is from a game I played more than 17 years ago and contains a combination that is still one of my favourites. It's against Evgeny Vladimirov from the 2004 Dubai Open, where I sort of half sacrificed, half blundered a pawn. But I have very good compensation with major development and potentially a very strong attack here.

In the game, he played **21...♕c6** and I retreated my queen with **22.♕e2** I then put the knight on h5, attacking g7 after he moved his bishop, and I broke through on the kingside to win a pretty nice game:
22...a5 23.♘h5 a4 24.♖hf1 ♖c7 25.♕f2 ♗c8 26.♕d4 ♖d7

27.♘xg7+ ♗xg7 28.♕xg7 ♖f8 29.♕xh6 b3 30.axb3 axb3 31.cxb3 ♗a6 32.♗xa6 ♕xa6

33.♕f4 ♖a7 34.♕b8+ ♔e7 35.♕b4+ 1-0.

'I can still remember how I was trembling with excitement, if instead he had played 21...♗c6'

But I can still remember how I was trembling with excitement, if instead he had played 21...♗c6.

Now my idea was to play 22.♕e2 and after he takes the rook with 22...♗xh1 I would capture on e6 with 23.♘xe6!.

ANALYSIS DIAGRAM

This all looks pretty dangerous for Black. If he takes the knight with 23...

The prize-giving of the 2004 Dubai Open, won by Shakhriyar Mamedyarov. Magnus Carlsen was one of 12 players to finish half a point behind the Azeri, which was good enough for his third and final Grandmaster norm.

it is impossible for Black to prevent the idea: if he moves the bishop back, 24...♗c6 or 24...♗b7, there is a check with 25.♖d8+

ANALYSIS DIAGRAM

and taking with either the queen or the rook will lead to the same result of 26.♘c7 and checkmate.

This is really one of the combinations that I'm very happy about. It is very aesthetic. This is something you usually would find in exercises and not in real games. I don't get to checkmate my opponent in every game, and I didn't get to do it in that game either; but just the 'feeling' of finding this combination was great. ∎

(This column is co-produced with Magnus Carlsen's 'Magnus Trainer' app . Download on Google Play, App Store, or visit play-magnus.com to read more lessons.)

fxe6, I will take back with 24.♕xe6+ and he will have to play 24...♗e7 and there will be a check with 25.♗g6+ and mate on the next move.

The only way for him to resist is to put his queen in between with 23...♕e7. Now none of my obvious options work, like taking on a6 with 24.♗xa6 as he'd simply take my knight with 24...♕xe6 and then the attack is over. So here again I need to be creative, and the feeling when I found the idea 24.♗f5!

ANALYSIS DIAGRAM

was just amazing. Still, the White threat might not be that obvious, but

Wesley So also wins Chessable Masters

American is only threat left for Magnus Carlsen in Champions Tour

OSLO

MINNETONKA, USA

In the studio in Oslo, Kaja Snare holds up the winner's belt that Wesley So will happily show to his friend Manny Pacquiao.

There is no denying that the Meltwater Champions Tour is dominated by Magnus Carlsen and Wesley So. In the absence of the World Champion, the American clinched his third victory in the penultimate leg, the Chessable Masters, to remain within striking distance of the overall leader. **ADHIBAN BASKARAN** shares his impressions.

It was a dreary day in Sochi when I was knocked out by Vidit Gujrathi in the third round. While I was trying to figure out what my next move in the chess world would be, I was lucky to get an invite to participate in the eighth leg of the Meltwater Champions Tour, the Chessable Masters! It was like a homecoming for me, as I just had made an epic course for Chessable about 1.b3, which I would say revolutionized chess in a way never seen before! (Yes, dear reader, the author is known to be shameless when it comes to promoting himself.)

Before we delve into what happened in the Chessable Masters, I would like to make a small excursion and think about the differences between over-the-board play and online chess. The advantages of the latter are clear. As World Champion Magnus Carlsen stated: 'It is interesting to play from the comfort of your home, and also organizers needn't worry about the financial costs of flight fares and hotel stays'. And so, despite the ongoing pants getting eliminated in three days, the preliminaries are bound to see plenty of drama. Perhaps the most dramatic game on the first day was between Jorden van Foreest and Levon Aronian, in which the latter blundered terribly and lost a winning position.

'Despite the ongoing pandemic, chess continued to grow thanks to the creation of the Champions Chess Tour'

pandemic, we have to be happy that chess evolved and continued to grow without signs of stopping, thanks to the creation of the Champions Chess Tour!

But there are disadvantages as well. There are times when you can lose a game without making any mistake, since, like nature, you can't control your internet ☺. Trust me, I am talking about this from personal experience. Despite having two separate net connections, there is no guarantee that it won't fail you at some time!

Still, in my personal opinion, these online events are one of the best things to happen for chess, and I hope it will continue to exist even after we find a way to fight this stupid virus!

The gruelling prelims
The field of the Chessable Masters was an exciting mix of old and new faces. Making their debut in the Champions Chess Tour were reigning Women's World Champion Ju Wenjun, India's Koneru Humpy, the youngest GM in the world, Abhimanyu Mishra, and Eduardo Iturrizaga from Venezuela.

The format was as we've become used to: 15 rounds spread over three days to reduce the number of players from 16 to eight, followed by the knock-out stage, with each stage consisting of two sets played over two days. With half of the partici-

Jorden van Foreest
Levon Aronian
CCT Chessable Masters 2021
(prelim-1)

position after 47...♖g2

Jorden van Foreest had gone for a crazy exchange sacrifice in an Italian game, but Levon Aronian defended well and managed to get an overwhelmingly winning advantage...
48.♔g1 Jorden had probably not been expecting the following gift... even in his wildest dreams!
48...f3??

49.g4+ A huge turnaround.
49...♔f4 50.♖xh2 ♔e3 51.bxc4 dxc4 52.♖b2
1-0. A very frustrating defeat for Levon! Nevertheless he managed to put this loss behind him and played the rest of the event very well.

On the second day, Shakhriyar Mamedyarov was on fire and won three games in a row. One of them was against young Abhi Mishra, twelve years old, as we all know!

Shakhriyar Mamedyarov
Abhimanyu Mishra
CCT Chessable Masters 2021
(prelim-9)
Sicilian Defence, Alapin Variation
1.e4 c5 2.c3 ♘f6 3.e5 ♘d5 4.♗c4 ♘b6 5.♗b3 d6 6.exd6 ♕xd6 7.♘f3 c4 8.♗c2 ♕e6+ 9.♔f1 g6 10.b3 ♗g7 11.♘a3 cxb3 12.axb3 0-0 13.d4 ♘c6

So far it was a safe game and true to his style, Mamedyarov starts his fireworks!
14.h4
The comp is not happy with the move, but to be honest, with a king on f1... this was begging to be played!
14...h5 15.♗g5 ♕d7
Strong was 15...♕d5!. 'The Art of Provocation', trying to get White to play c4, which weakens his centre or else Black can strongly continue with ...♗g4!. This would have given Abhi the advantage.
16.♕e1
A deep move, preparing to bring the a1-rook into play.

16...e6? A huge mistake. It wasn't a good idea to close the c8-h3 diagonal, and this also seriously weakens Black's dark squares on the kingside.
17.♖d1 Mamedyarov could have got a big advantage with 17.♖h3, followed by ♖g3, with a strong attack and a kingside initiative.
17...♘d5 Abhi is trying to fianchetto the bishop, but it turns out to be very slow and time-consuming.
18.c4 ♘db4 19.♗e4 a5 20.♘b5 b6 Finally... But at what cost??

21.♘e5 ♕b7 The alternative was to give up the g7-bishop, which wouldn't have changed anything!

22.g4! White's strategy falls into place and Black can no longer defend against the attack!

22...hxg4 23.h5 f5 24.♗g2 ♗xe5 25.dxe5 ♕h7 26.♕d2 gxh5 27.♗h6

Preparing ♖xh5 or ♕g5+.
27...♖f7 28.♕d8+!
A beautiful way to finish the game!
28...♘xd8 29.♖xd8+ ♖f8 30.♖xf8 Mate.

Although Black had chances to defend against the attack and gain

an advantage, full credit to Mamedyarov for a clean display once he got the chance!

Let's take a look at a game between two of the debutants on the second day. Eduardo Iturrizaga and Ju Wenjun decided to engage in a tactical skirmish, which only one of them could win!

Eduardo Iturrizaga
Ju Wenjun
CCT Chessable Masters 2021
(prelim-9)

position after 25...♖f6

26.♕e2!? Iturrizaga wants to maintain control of the e-file, and Jun Wenjun possibly felt that he had missed a tactical detail... But she found out the truth the hard way.
26...♖xb2 27.♖e8+ ♔h7

28.♘g5+! A cool detail, which was probably foreseen by Itu!
28...hxg5 Since 28...♔g6 29.h5 is mate. **29.♕h5+ ♖h6 30.♕f7** Ju is forced to give up the queen.
30...♕xe8 30...♕f6 31.♕g8+ ♔g6 32.♖e6, winning the queen.
31.♕xe8 ♖xh4

CCT Chessable Classic 2021 (prelims)

			Elo rapid		TPR
1	Wesley So	USA	2741	11	2818
2	Levon Aronian	ARM	2778	10½	2791
3	Alireza Firouzja	FRA	2703	10½	2796
4	Hikaru Nakamura	USA	2829	10½	2787
5	Vladislav Artemiev	RUS	2769	9½	2737
6	Le Quang Liem	VIE	2744	9	2716
7	Shakhriyar Mamedyarov	AZE	2761	9	2715
8	Jorden van Foreest	NED	2543	8½	2701
9	Adhiban Baskaran	IND	2624	7	2637
10	Eduardo Iturrizaga	ESP	2635	7	2636
11	Aryan Tari	NOR	2519	6½	2622
12	Pentala Harikrishna	IND	2705	6	2581
13	David Anton	ESP	2667	5½	2560
14	Ju Wenjun	CHN	2610	5	2542
15	Abhimanyu Mishra	USA	2340	2½	2406
16	Humpy Koneru	IND	2483	2	2362

32.♗f3 The only way to keep the advantage was 32.♖e1!. **32...♖h3** Suddenly Black is back in the game! Ju has enough counterplay to hold the balance. **33.♗d5 gxf4 34.♖e1**

34...♖g3+ Missing the chance... Ju had to find 34...♘e5! 35.♖xe5 ♗xe5 36.♛xe5 ♖g3+ 37.♔f1 ♖b1+, followed by a forced perpetual! **35.♔f1**

No more tricks and White is winning again! **35...♗f6 36.♛h5+ ♔g7 37.♛f7+ ♔h6 38.♛xf6+** 1-0.

While on the third day of the prelims the 'favourites' qualified easily, the final chase was between me and Jorden van Foreest! I took a slight lead by winning the first game of the day against Abhimanyu Mishra.

After he had been eliminated from the World Cup, Adhiban was relieved to be invited to the Chessable Masters so he could continue promoting his Lifetime Repertoire course on 1.b3.

Adhiban Baskaran
Abhimanyu Mishra
CCT Chessable Masters 2021
(prelim-11)

position after 12...d5

13.e5!? Making a mess of things!
13...♘fd7 13...♛xe5 14.0-0-0 leads to a large advantage for White.
14.♘gf5!? Raising the stakes!
14...exf5 15.e6

15...♘e5

This turns out to be too slow.
Abhi should have gone for 15...fxe6! 16.♘xe6 ♛e5 17.gxf5 ♘c5! (immediately challenging the powerful knight on e6!) 18.0-0-0 ♘xe6 19.fxe6 ♖f8, with a clear advantage to Black, now that my main trump card and the source of my compensation, the beautiful e6-knight, is no more!
Also quite strong was 15...0-0 16.exd7 ♘xd7, with advantage for Black.
16.exf7+ ♘xf7 17.♘e6 ♛e5 18.gxf5
The knight reigns supreme on e6!
18...♘d6 19.0-0-0 d4
And now I missed the chance to create an attacking masterpiece!

20.♗a4+ After 20.♛xb7!! ♘xb7 21.♗xd4 White is a full queen down, but he's still winning due to Black's sleeping army and weak king! 21...♛e4 22.♗xg7! (threatening checkmate on c7!) 22...♘d7 23.♗d5

ANALYSIS DIAGRAM

followed by ♗xh8, with a winning advantage and a continuing attack.
20...♘d7 21.♕h5+ g6 22.♗xd4
I found a slightly different way to give up the queen ☺!
22...gxh5 It wasn't easy to see 22...♕a5, which both of us had missed! After 23.♕e2 ♕xa4 24.♗xh8 the computer follows up with a forced sequence starting with 24...♖c8! that leads to an equal endgame (of course).
23.♗xe5 Now I have a clear plus after all the skirmishing! **23...♗xh1**

24.♗xh8
24.♖xh1! ♖g8 25.♖d1 would have led to a bigger advantage.
24...♗f3 25.♖g1 ♘xf5 26.♘c7+ ♔d8 27.♘xa8 ♗xa8 28.♖g8+ ♘f8 29.♗f6

The last tactical trick, leading to an endgame with an extra exchange and two extra pawns, which I converted (1-0, 47). One of the craziest games of the prelims!

Unfortunately, for me, I also suffered two losses against Firouzja and So, and could not catch up with Jorden. Even if I had won my last game against Aronian, it would not have made a difference, but disheartened I ended up losing a winning game!

One of Kramnik's famous statements was 'Chess is an art' and the following design created by my compatriot Harikrishna is testament to that!

Pentala Harikrishna
Ju Wenjun
CCT Chessable Masters 2021
(prelim-12)

position after 17.♖ac1

Harikrishna had achieved a solid advantage, so Ju Wenjun decided it was time to create some counterplay using the pressure along the a5-e1 diagonal.
17...exd4 18.cxd4 d5 19.e5 ♘e4 20.♘xe4!

I have never seen such a pretty example showing the power of the bishops and a strong pawn centre!

There were other ways, but this looks the most convincing and certainly the most colourful way to gain an advantage with a thematic exchange sacrifice!
20...dxe4 21.♗xe4 ♗xe1 22.♘xe1 ♘a5 23.♕h5 Preparing the nasty ♗xh6. **23...♖b6 24.d5 ♖a6 25.♘f3 ♘c4 26.♗d4**

I have never seen such a pretty example showing the power of the bishops and a strong pawn centre! There was no doubt as to the result of the game once such a beautiful design in the centre of the board was achieved!! (Hari won in another 8 moves, but I prefer to end the game here ☺). [The final moves were: 26...♕e7 27.♖e1 ♕f8 28.♗c3 ♕e7 29.♗d3 ♗c8 30.♘d4 ♘xe5 31.♗xb5 g6 32.♕xh6 ♖f6 33.♗xe8 ♕xe8 34.♕g5 1-0 – ed.]

The knock-out stage
In the quarter final, Jorden was paired against top-favourite Wesley So. After surviving a worse position in the first game, Jorden drew first blood in the second game. In a very destructive demolition of the Berlin he ended Wesley's unbeaten streak in the tournament.

Jorden van Foreest
Wesley So
CCT Chessable Masters 2021
(qf 1.2)

Ruy Lopez, Berlin Defence

**1.e4 e5 2.♘f3 ♘c6 3.♗b5 ♘f6
4.d3 ♗c5 5.♗g5!?**

Commentators David Howell and Jovanka Houska can barely believe it,
Jorden van Foreest is crushing Wesley So in under 20 moves.

5...♘e7 Wesley wasn't expecting Jorden's direction and chooses a very risky way to neutralize the pin along the h4-d8 diagonal.
5...h6 6.♗h4 d6 is the most popular way for Black, leading to complex positions.
6.♗xf6 gxf6 7.d4!
Continuing to play with great vigour to break up Black's pawn structure before he can set up his centre with ...c6/...d6/...♘g6.
7...exd4 8.0-0

Now that Black's pawn structure is a wreck, it was time to castle ☺!
8...c6 9.♗c4 0-0
A risky decision. Surprisingly, the king was maybe safer on e8!
Wesley had to look for counter-chances via the g-file with 9...♖g8.
10.♘xd4 d6 11.♘c3 f5 12.♕d2
An interesting decision, and Wesley had to find the only way to survive!

12...♔h8 This natural move leaves Jorden clearly in control.
The only way was 12...f4!, with the idea of playing ...♘g6: 13.♘b3 ♘g6 14.♘xc5 dxc5 15.♕xd8 ♖xd8, with an equal game, as the pawn structure doesn't matter so much, since 'we are in the endgame now!'.
13.♖ad1
Bringing in the reserves while Black is struggling to organize his army.
13...♗b6 14.♘f3!

Slowly but surely, the attack is building up!
14...fxe4 14...♘g6 was more stubborn, although White has a clean extra pawn after 15.♕xd6.
15.♘xe4 ♘f5 16.g4!
Zero hesitation!
**16...♘g7 17.♕h6 ♗xg4 18.♘fg5
♗f5 19.♘xd6** 1-0.

A powerful display by Jorden, and I even thought that this game might be the key to him beating Wesley; but it was not to be. Wesley struck back on the same day with a new idea in the King's Indian g3 system, equalized the score, and followed up with a strong performance on the next day and moving to the next stage of the event.

Among the other quarter-final match-ups, Nakamura vs Artemiev was a bloodbath. They kept trading blows by winning with the white pieces and ultimately Artemiev prevailed in the Armageddon. Artemiev took his win philosophically: 'Armageddon is a different story; it's more nerves and more about luck, I think'.

The match between Le Quang Liem and Alireza Firouzja was a remarkably one-sided affair. Liem was clearly in great form, and after winning the first day, he also went on to win the first two games of the second day, prematurely ending the match by delivering one of the most dominant eliminations in the Chessable Masters! This is how he put a definitive end to any hopes the Frenchman still might have had.

Le Quang Liem
Alireza Firouzja
CCT Chessable Masters 2021
(qf 1.4)
Queen's Pawn Game

1.d4 ♘f6 2.♘f3 c5
Liem had convincingly outplayed Firouzja in the Catalan, so now

Alireza tries to drum up trouble with a complicated line!
3.d5 b5 4.e4!

Showing no fear and going for a cool pawn sacrifice to punish Black for his development issues.
4...♘xe4 5.♗d3 ♕a5+
An important intermezzo before withdrawing the knight.
Safer was 5...♘f6, giving up the pawn and hoping to finish his development, although after 6.♗xb5 g6 7.♘c3 ♗g7 8.0-0 0-0 9.d6! White is clearly better, while Black has to somehow find counterplay, which isn't trivial.
6.♘bd2

6...♘d6
The other retreat, 6...♘f6, is met by 7.0-0 c4 8.♗e4 d6 9.a4!, with good chances to gain a big advantage.
7.0-0 c4 8.♘e4!
The key move, which gives White a winning advantage, something that Liem probably knew beforehand!

8...♘xe4
Or 8...cxd3 9.♘xd6+ exd6 10.♖e1+ ♔d8 11.♘g5, with a winning attack – just look at Black's sleeping army ☺!
9.♗xe4 d6 10.♘d4

White had achieved a winning advantage, which he confidently converted! (1-0, 32)

The quarter-final match between Levon Aronian and Shakhriyar

BEREND VONK

Mamedyarov was fun for the spectators, but not for Mamed. Because he kept missing his chances, his opponent managed to survive many lost positions, finally winning the encounter without any playoffs!

After Levon Aronian had already prevailed 2½-½ on the first day, this was how their second day started.

Shakhriyar Mamedyarov
Levon Aronian
CCT Chessable Masters 2021
(qf 2.1)

position after 33...♕b8

34.♖xf7+! The best way to convert!
34...♔xf7 35.♕h6!
Preparing the deadly ♘g5+.
35...♕g8 36.♘g5+ ♔e7 37.♘xe4 fxe4 Here Mamedyarov had to find the only way to keep his advantage...

38.♖e1
Losing an important pawn!
Correct was the safe and intuitive 38.♖c1!, protecting the c4-pawn, with a large advantage, as the activity of the queen combined with the pawns on the kingside should be enough to win the game.
38...♕xc4

Black is out of danger and White can only equalize here...
39.♕g5 Better was 39.g4!?, creating counterplay, which helps to keep the balance. **39...d3** The pawns become unstoppable! **40.♔g2 ♕d4 41.♕xg6 c4 42.♕g7+ ♔e6**

The knight is a fantastic defender and stops the checks from the queen.
43.♕c7 d2 44.♖d1 c3 45.g4 e3 46.♕c6+ ♔e7 47.♕b7+ ♔d7
0-1. An unfortunate loss for Mamedyarov.

Mamedyarov did win the next game, but another victory took Aronian into the semi-finals.

Survival of the fittest
In the semi-final match against Vladislav Artemiev, Wesley won a single game and drew the rest on Day 1. Next he thwarted Artemiev's attempts on Day 2, thanks to the following game. Even Artemiev praised his opponent for his near-flawless play: 'He played fantastically, I think, because I watched a little bit and the computer says that every move by Wesley was strong – maybe the first line or second line.'

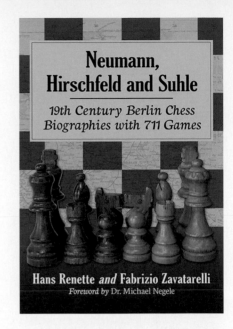
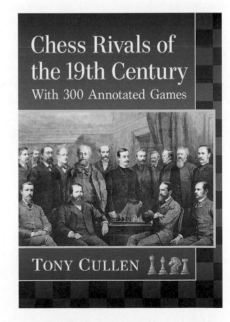

Not fearing any ghosts and not wasting any time on niceties like ♗d2.
11...♗xc3 12.bxc3 ♘8e7 13.♗d3 b5 14.♖hf1! Wesley is clearly on top in this game., All his moves are matching the comp's!
14...♘d5 15.♗d2 ♗b7 16.♖de1 ♘ge7 17.f5

And Wesley had a very strong initiative, which he converted into a large advantage; large enough to win the game (1-0, 33), and the match!

The other semi-final, between Levon Aronian and Le Quang Liem, remained tense till the very end. Liem won the first set, but Levon hit back in the second and an Armageddon game had to decide. Levon had to choose the colour and, just like Nakamura, once again choose Black rather than be White and have extra time. This is something I'll never understand ☺. It was a crazy game, in which both players had their chances before they liquidated into a drawn endgame. With no time increments until move 61, anything seemed possible, and then Aronian lost on time on move 69 in a drawn position.

Vladislav Artemiev showed inspired chess, but in the semi-finals the Russian had to bow to a superior Wesley So.

Wesley So
Vladislav Artemiev
CCT Chessable Masters 2021
(sf 2.2)
Sicilian Defence, Taimanov Variation
1.e4 c5 2.♘f3 e6 3.d4 cxd4 4.♘xd4 ♘c6 5.♘c3 ♕c7 6.♗e3 a6 7.♕f3 ♘e5 8.♕g3

8...♗d6 In a topical line Artemiev goes for a slightly risky direction, which could prove successful, only if... 8...h5 is the mainly tested line that has been well explored and the final word is not out yet!
9.f4!
Wesley goes for the most principled approach, ignoring the gift on g7. 9.♕xg7 runs into 9...♘g6 10.♘f3 f6! 11.♘d4 (preventing ...♗f8 due to the discovered attack via the second rank with ♘xe6!) 11...♕b8. Moving away from the threat and preparing ...♗f8. It does look like the end for the queen, but White has a trump card up his sleeve... 12.e5!

ANALYSIS DIAGRAM

The only way to save the queen! After 12...♗f8 13.exf6 ♗xg7 14.fxg7 White has full compensation for the queen, as was seen in Jakubowski-Chigaev, Titled Tuesday 2021.
9...♘g6 10.e5 ♗b4 11.0-0-0

The Final

Both Wesley So and Le Quang Liem had survived tough ordeals to reach the final and both had shown some great chess. It was not easy to make a prediction, but Wesley proved ruthless on the first day, winning both games as White and remaining solid on the black side. This is from Game 3, in which he completely demolished Liem.

Wesley So
Le Quang Liem
CCT Chessable Masters 2021
(sf 1.3)

position after 21...♘c5

A topical line of the complex Zaitsev Variation in the Ruy Lopez, and here Wesley introduces a less explored direction...
22.b3!? ♘bd3
The most natural reply!
23.♗xd3 ♘xd3 24.♖e3
The rooks on a3 and e3 look funny!
24...b4 24...♕g6 was more accurate, leading to a balanced game.
25.♖a1 ♘e5

26.♘xe5
This looks natural, but it allows Black

to equalize and even take over the initiative/advantage.
Wesley had to find the computer-like 26.a5!, making sure that the b4-pawn would not get moral support from the a6-pawn and remain an easy target for the white pieces, with a clear advantage.
26...dxe5 27.♘f5

27...c3
Missing his chance and giving White the opportunity to reclaim his advantage!
Black had to challenge White's strong knight on f5 with 27...♗c8!, yielding a slight pull.
28.♖f3!
A cool move, after which Black's position suddenly falls apart and becomes indefensible!
28...♕d8
28...♕b6 is met by 29.♗e3, kicking the queen away from the 3rd rank, with the idea of taking on h6, as in the game!
29.♘xh6+! gxh6 30.♖g3+ ♔h7
30...♗g7 31.♗xh6 wins easily.
31.♕g4

Black resigned.

Liem started strongly on the second day of the final by winning in a chaotic battle in the boring London System, in which Wesley missed his fair share of winning chances! Just when it looked as if Liem was all set to force a playoff, Wesley found a hole in his repertoire and uncorked a stunning concept that questions White's entire strategy!

Le Quang Liem
Wesley So
CCT Chessable Masters 2021
(final 2.3)
Queen's Pawn Game
1.d4 ♘f6 2.♘f3 d5 3.e3

One of Liem's patent lines for this event, which he used successfully against Levon Aronian. His other favourite line would be 3.c3 ☺.
3...c5 4.dxc5 e6 5.b4 a5
The best reply! After 5...b6 White can go for 6.cxb6 ♗xb4+ 7.c3, keeping the extra pawn, with good chances of gaining an edge.
6.c3 axb4 7.cxb4 b6

8.♗b5+
8.a4 bxc5 9.b5 is another direction, but one which is not computer-approved!

9...c4 10.♗e2 ♘bd7 was seen in So-Carlsen, chess.com blitz 2017.
8...♗d7 9.♗xd7+ ♘bxd7 10.a4 bxc5 11.b5
White is trying to play a Noteboom type of game with reversed colours, and it was Liem's bad luck that Firouzja had already played this system to beat Wesley... So Wesley was in no mood to let that happen again and was well prepared to meet this line with an explosive concept!

11...g5!
More or less ending White's career in this line! Black takes control of the kingside play, leaving White struggling with space and finding a plan... After 11...♗d6 12.♗b2 0-0 13.0-0 ♕c7 14.♘bd2 c4 15.♗c3 White was already better and went on to win in Firouzja-So, Skilling Rapid 2020.
12.♗b2 ♗d6 13.♕e2 g4 14.♘fd2 ♕c7

15.f4 Fighting back to get some control, but unfortunately, this break only helps Black!
15.e4! was more tenacious, and possibly White can equalize with accurate play.
15...gxf3 16.♘xf3 ♖g8

Black has achieved a slight advantage and easy play for his pieces, utilizing the g-file and control of the e4-square, which is a juicy outpost for the knight.
17.0-0 ♔e7

The king is feeling very safe here! 17...♖g4 was slightly more precise, retaining the advantage.
18.♘bd2 It was important to get the queenside pawns rolling with 18.♗c3, followed by a5.
18...♖g4!

Now Wesley is firmly in control!
19.♕d1
How else to defend the a4-pawn?
19...♖ag8 20.♖f2 ♖b4!

An epic way to prepare ...♘g4 (or

...♘e4, as it turns out) with tempo.
21.♘f1 ♘e4 22.♖c2 ♕a7 23.♕e1 ♘ef6
Stopping any ♕h4 ideas.
24.♗xf6+ ♖xf6 25.♖ca2 ♖gg4
The pressure on the a4-pawn is mounting.
26.♕d1 ♖gc4
This was a very funny placement for the rooks on b4/c4 – not something I have seen before!
26...♘e4 was stronger, followed by ...f5.
27.♘3d2 ♖c3 28.♖b1 c4 29.a5 ♖xb1 30.♕xb1

30...♗c5
Here Wesley had to find 30...♕c5! to keep the advantage! 31.a6 d4! Black's attack is faster! One sample line is 32.a7 dxe3 33.a8♕ exd2+ 34.♔h1 ♖c1, when the extra queen doesn't

CCT Chessable Classic (KO finals)			
Quarter Final			
So-Van Foreest	2-2	2½-½	
Nakamura-Artemiev	2-2	2-2	1-2
Firouzja-Le Quang Liem	1-3	0-2	
Aronian-Mamedyarov	2½-½	2-1	
Semi-Final			
So-Artemiev	2½-1½	2-2	
Aronian-Le Quang Liem	1-3	2½-1½	1-2
Final 3rd-4th place			
Aronian-Artemiev	2-2	½-2½	
Final			
So-Le Quang Liem	2½-½	2-2	

Now the b-pawn is firmly under control and Black's queen is free to wreak havoc!

38.♖b2 ♕e5!

A very strong idea, using the fact that White's king is in big danger, thanks to the combined forces of queen and bishop!

39.♖xb3 cxb3 The pawn is untouchable due to the mating threat on e4.

40.♘d2 ♕e3 41.♕c1 b2! 42.♕c7+ ♔f6 43.♕f4+ ♕xf4 44.gxf4 ♔f5

The rest is easy, as Wesley has just way too many pawns...

45.♔g2 ♔xf4 46.♔f1 ♔e3 47.♔e1 ♔d3 48.♔d1 f5

White resigned.

An important victory, which was followed by a solid draw in the next round, which assured Wesley So of the title.

With this victory, Wesley has won three Champions Chess Tour finals. In his own words, he 'just wanted to make sure that World Champion Magnus Carlsen is forced to show up' for the final leg, the Aimchess US Rapid.

The battle in the overall standings is clearly between the two of them, with Magnus Carlsen fairly comfortably in the lead with 291 points and Wesley So in second place with 257 points. The gap between them and the rest is huge, with Levon Aronian (3rd, 149), Teimour Radjabov (4th, 133) and Anish Giri (5th, 123) far behind. ∎

change the assessment and Black is clearly winning.

31.b6

Suddenly the pawns are a force to be reckoned with!

31...♕b8 32.b7

In a practical game, I think this is a big error, since the pawns can easily be blocked by the bishop on a7 now.

Stronger was 32.h3!, stopping ...♘g4 ideas, and White keeps some chances to gain the advantage.

32...♘g4

Now the game is balanced.

33.g3 ♘xe3 34.a6 ♗a7 35.♔h1 ♖d3 36.♘xe3 ♖xe3 37.♘f1

An error that allows Black to find the winning move!

37.♕b4+ would have kept the balance.

37...♖b3!

Wesley So 'just wanted to make sure that World Champion Magnus Carlsen is forced to show up' for the final leg

MAXIMize your Tactics
with Maxim Notkin

Find the best move in the positions below

Solutions on page 89

1. Black to play

2. Black to play

3. White to play

4. Black to play

5. Black to play

6. Black to play

7. White to play

8. Black to play

9. White to play

GIBRALTAR
BATTLE OF THE SEXES

JANUARY 24TH TO FEBRUARY 3RD

2022

SPONSORED BY

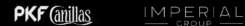

Judit Polgar

Elementary endgame fortresses

Most chess players like to attack, but defending well can also yield many points. In this first article in a series on various defensive approaches, **JUDIT POLGAR** looks at endgame fortresses that can salvage seemingly hopeless positions.

The complex process of winning a game often consists of two main phases. To begin with, the winner needs to establish a sufficiently large positional or material advantage, which then needs to be converted into a win.

From a philosophical point of view, the first part seems to be more important and more difficult to achieve: in order to break the initial (near-) equality, one needs to outplay one's opponent in more ways than one. Having achieved this, one is not there yet, and we need to remember that winning a won position is an art – at which almost all elite players from different eras excelled.

Many players relax their focus or lose some of their motivation after reaching a winning position. Since everything seems to be winning, they often start playing without a plan. In many cases, this allows the defender to save the game, sometimes in quite surprising ways.

Having established an overwhelming material advantage, one of the easiest things to overlook is the defender's ability to set up a remarkably strong fortress.

There are two possible situations:
1. The weaker side does not allow the enemy king (or other important pieces) to penetrate its camp.
2. He does not allow the king to get out of a restricted area.

I will illustrate both situations with the help of two fascinating studies.

Chekhover 1947
White to move and draw

The situation looks trivial. The white king is apparently forced to stop the a-pawn, allowing Black to advance on the kingside with decisive effect. However, there is a subtle way in which to establish a reliable fortress. The trump cards that White should build his defence on are his compact structure and his potentially strong bishop – strengths that can be used to throw up a long barrier by combining the control on the light and dark squares.

1.f3! Not just a consolidating move, as we will see.

White is too late to create counterplay: 1.♗h2 a4 2.♔d2 a3 3.♔c2 ♔g5 4.f4+ exf4 5.e5 a2 6.♔b2 f3 7.exd6 (7.♗g1 f2 8.♗xf2 h2 won't change anything) 7...f2 wins for Black.

1...a4 2.♔f2!!

The second step on the way to reaching perfect coordination.

Winning a won position is an art, at which almost all elite players from different eras excelled

2.♔d2 won't save White: 2...♔g5 3.♗e3+ ♔h4 4.♗f2+ ♔h5! (staying close to h4) 5.♗g1 h2! (clearing the king's path) 6.♗xh2 ♔h4 (threatening ...♔h3, followed by ...♔g3) 7.f4 (White's only chance) 7...a3 8.♔c2 a2 9.♔b2 exf4 10.e5 f3 11.♗g1 ♔g3 12.exd6 f2 13.♗xf2+ ♔xf2 14.dxc7 a1♕+ 15.♔xa1 g1♕+, and wins.
2...a3 3.♔g3 Continuing the mysterious regrouping.
3...a2 4.♔xh3 a1♕ 5.♔xg2

Amazingly enough, Black will be unable to win this. The bishop does a wonderful job. It defends the king against attacks along the first rank, prevents the enemy king from being transferred via the a-file, and together with the white king it can also prevent any invasion via f4.
5...♕b2+ 6.♗f2 ♔g5 7.♔g3 ♕c1 8.♗a7!

The only move, but sufficiently effective.
8...♕f4+ 9.♔g2 Black has found the only way to push the white king back, but now the f4-square is unavailable to invading forces.
9...♔h4 10.♗f2+ And Black cannot make progress. ½-½.

One of the easiest things to overlook is the defender's ability to set up a remarkably strong fortress

In the next example, too, Black will reach a position with a queen versus a minor piece, but his king will be 'neutralized' on a passive square just in time.

Troitzky 1910
White to play and draw

The knight is hanging and the d-pawn is ready to run. Does White have any chance to draw?
1.♘c6!
Moving closer to the pawn and attacking the bishop.
At first sight, 1.♘d7? seems simpler. After 1...d3 2.♘f6 d2? 3.g3+ ♔g5 4.♘e4+ White eliminates the pawn,

Alexey Troitzky (1866-1942), one of the greatest endgame study composers of all time.

but the intermediate check 2...♗b8!+, followed by ...d3-d2, will win.
1...d3 2.♘xa7!!
Surprisingly enough, eliminating the bishop saves White.
After 2.♘e5 d2 3.f4, threatening both g2-g3 mate and ♘f3+, followed by ♘xd2, the bishop once again reveals its strength with 3...♗g1+!, dismantling White's mechanism before promoting the pawn.
2...d2

The knight has lost the race by one tempo. However, this is not a race, it is face-to-face combat!
3.♘b5! d1♕ 4.♘c3!!
Attacking the queen and planning ♘e4, dominating the black king.
4...♕d6+ Amazingly, Black does not increase his chances by gaining a tempo with this check.
5.♔h1! But not 5.♔g1?? ♕c5+, winning the knight.

5...♕e6 Quite sadly, the king has no time to escape, since both 5...♔g5?? 6.♘e4+ and 5...♔g3?? 6.♘e4+ win the queen.
6.♘e4 The black king has been immobilized, and the queen cannot

cause any damage by itself. White will never find himself in zugzwang, since the king has three squares at its disposal (h2, h1 and g1). For instance:

6...♛e5 7.♔g1 ♛a1+ 8.♔h2

Black controls two of the aforementioned squares, but cannot make a waiting move along the first rank, since this would allow g2-g3 mate! This means he has to pin the pawn, allowing the white king to retreat.

8...♛b2 9.♔h1

With a positional draw.

Don't give up too soon

I will never get tired of preaching about how useful it is to solve endgame studies on a regular basis.

Solving studies teaches one that one should never give up too soon

This habit improves one's calculating powers, widens one's imagination and develops one's perseverance. The latter can also be formulated differently: solving studies teaches one that one should never give up too soon.

In the next two examples, the black players failed to cope with far simpler over-the-board situations.

I remember arriving in Wijk aan Zee (as a guest) in 2019, just a few minutes after the following game had come to an abrupt finish.

Anish Giri
Sam Shankland
Wijk aan Zee 2019

position after 38...♔d7

The white king is very active and the bishop enjoys better mobility than the knight. These elements put Black in serious danger.

39.♗f8 ♘h4 40.♗xh6 ♘f3 41.h3

Inviting the knight to move to the square where it will be imprisoned.

41...♘g1 42.♗xg5 ♘xh3 43.♗e3

White has achieved his first aim, and the knight is doomed. However, this does not guarantee a win!

43...♔d6 44.♔f5 ♔d5

45.b6!?

A psychologically inspired move, seeming to kill Black positionally.

45.♔g4 fails to trap the knight due to 45...♔e4, forcing the bishop to give up its domination.

Giri refrained from the slightly more consistent 45.♗c5, probably suspecting that Shankland would have been able to calculate the few simple lines leading to a draw: 45...b6! (a forced way to eliminate the rest of the pawns) 46.♗xb6 ♔c4 47.♗c5 ♔xb5 48.♔g4 ♘f2+, with a draw.

Giri was aware of the fact that the endgame was drawn, but played his last move – dooming the knight without offering Black any queenside counterplay – very confidently, as if he was sure he would win. This little psychological trick worked out well. Sam was convinced by Giri's body language and... resigned.

If he had known (or remembered) a well-known theoretical position, he would have played 45...♔d6. Without the b4-pawn this is a well-known fortress. The only way White can put pressure on Black is... by stalemating him, since there is no room to penetrate left of the b-pawns. The extra pawn does not change anything, of course. The thematic lines go 46.♔g4 ♔d7 47.♔xh3 ♔c8 48.♗f4 ♔d7 49.♔g4 ♔c8 50.♔f5 ♔d7 51.♔f6 ♔c8

ANALYSIS DIAGRAM

52.♗e3 (52.♗e7 is stalemate) 52...♔b8 53.♔e6 ♔a8 54.♔d7 ♔b8 55.♔d8 ♔a8 56.♗c8, stalemating again.

Using common sense

Endgames arise after a complex opening and middlegame, usually full of important events and ups and downs. This episode shows that in such circumstances, even strong grandmasters find it difficult to switch their mind-set to remembering basic knowledge of critical endgame positions.

The situation was a bit more complicated in the next example, but if unfamiliar with the theoretical endgame in question, Black should have saved the game by using his common sense.

Fabiano Caruana
Maxime Vachier-Lagrave
Yekaterinburg Candidates 2021

position after 55.♖d3

With the pawn on g4, Black's defence would be easier, but the way it is, the rook check on g3 can cause serious trouble. Vachier-Lagrave played the losing move:

55...♘h6? And although Caruana later gave him another chance to save the game, Black eventually lost.

The correct way of setting up the fortress was with 55...♘g7!. Many commentators considered this a 'deep computer move', but the simple truth is that this idea was known long before the advent of computers. The knight and the pawn create a long barrier to stop the white king. In the game Schmidt-Urban, Gdansk 1994, this is precisely how Black defended and reached a draw. The only differ-

Many considered this a 'deep computer move', but this idea was known long before the advent of computers

ence is that in that game the position was mirrored, so instead of 55...♘g7 Black played 71...♘b7.

White's only chance to make progress (after 55...♘g7) is bringing the king to e7, which is the only breach in Black's fortress:

ANALYSIS DIAGRAM

56.♖g3+ ♔f7 57.♔e4 ♔f8 58.♔d5 ♔f7 59.♖g4 ♔f8 60.♔d6 ♔f7 61.♖a4

ANALYSIS DIAGRAM

White has made some progress, and this is a good moment for Black to think of counterplay, since the white king is far from the g2-pawn. 61...♘f5+ 62.♔d7 ♘e3 63.♖a2 f5, with drawing counterplay.

Conclusions

■ One should solve studies on a regular basis and polish one's endgame knowledge and understanding.

■ In apparently desperate positions, when facing the imminent danger of suffering an overwhelming material disadvantage, one should immediately search for ways to set up a fortress.

■ Knowledge of elementary theoretical drawn positions and general patterns is indispensable in the endgame. Over time, it may save many points! ■

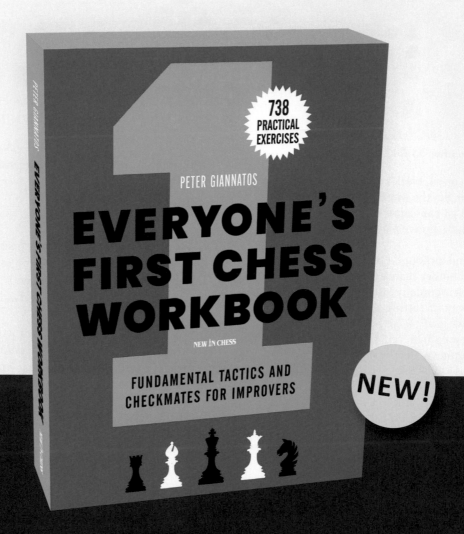

Thomas Willemze

Club players, test your decision-making skills!

What would you play?

What is your plan? What are you looking for? One approach is to look for the weak spots in your opponent's position and direct your forces there.

I f you are in need of a constructive plan in your games, you can start with assessing your position and try to gradually improve it as much as possible – for instance by moving your worst-placed piece to a better square. Another approach is to develop a nose for weaknesses in your opponent's camp and try to exploit those where you can.

Exercises

The entertaining clash between Jozef Hujo (1926) and Miroslav Holicky (1794) was played in the Slovakia Open in Piestany, a well-known spa town some 90 kilometres from the capital Bratislava. The game was full of instructive moments in which vulnerable pawns, squares and pieces played important parts. I created four exercises that can help you improve your sense for the weakest spot in your opponent's camp.

Exercise 1

position after 14.b3

Black has almost finished his development and can now choose between

several appealing pawn breaks. Would you advance on the queenside with **14...a5** and 15...a4, target the g4-pawn with **14...h5**, or prepare a central pawn break with **14...♘d7** ?

Exercise 2

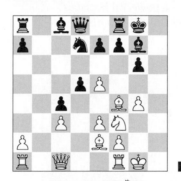

position after 19.♘f3

Black has several options for attacking a vulnerable white pawn. What should he do? Go after the e5-pawn with **19...♕b6** and 20...♕e6, attack the g4-pawn with **19...♘c5**, or open up the long diagonal with **19...f6** to target the c3-pawn?

Exercise 3

position after 22...♗b7

White has to find a way to deal with the attack on his rook. Would you withdraw the rook with **23.♖d1**, keep it on the fifth rank with **23.♖a5**, or simply ignore the attack with **23.♗xc4** ?

Exercise 4

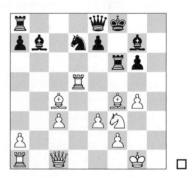

position after 23...♔f8

Both players have moved since the last exercise, and the white rook is still under attack. What would you play? Support both rook and knight with **24.♕d1**, attack the black rook with **24.g5**, or send the knight on a mission with **24.♘g5** ?

I hope you enjoyed these exercises and were able to identify and exploit the most promising weaknesses in the enemy camp. You can find the full analysis of this game below.

Try to exploit the weaknesses in your opponent's camp!

Jozef Hujo (1926)
Miroslav Holicky (1794)
Piestany, Slovakia Open 2021
Queen's Pawn Opening, London System

1.d4 d5 2.♗f4 ♘f6 3.e3 c5 4.♘f3 ♘c6 5.c3 ♕b6 6.♕b3 c4 7.♕c2

7...♗f5

This is a standard tactic in this structure. The point is that 8.♕xf5 will run into 8...♕xb2, trapping the rook.

8.♕c1

The queen has already moved three times in the opening. It did, however, lure the black c-pawn to c4, which removes the pressure on the d4-pawn and gives White b2-b3 as a potential pawn break in the future.

8...g6

With the a1-h8 diagonal obstructed by the rock-solid b2-c3-d4-pawn chain, Black usually develops the bishop with 8...e6.

9.♘bd2 ♗g7 10.h3

10...♕d8

By freeing the b-pawn and protecting the rook, Black is now able to answer 11.b3 with the thematic 11...b5 12.a4 a6. However, simply finishing development with 10...0-0! would

have been a much more effective way to prevent this typical pawn break. White is now behind in development and it would be ill-advised for him to open up the position: after 11.b3 cxb3 12.axb3 ♖fc8

ANALYSIS DIAGRAM

Black will follow up with 13...♘e4 and have a powerful initiative.

11.♗e2 0-0 12.0-0 b5

13.g4

White lacks a concrete follow-up to justify this committal move. He should have focused on the queenside first with 13.a4.

ANALYSIS DIAGRAM

Black is facing a tough choice here. 13...b4 would allow White to stir up

the centre with 14.♘e5 ♘xe5 15.dxe5 ♘d7 16.e4!, and the more prudent 13...a6 is met by 14.b3!.

ANALYSIS DIAGRAM

Both 14...cxb3 15.axb5! and 14...bxa4 15.bxc4! are out of the question, which means that White can slowly but surely improve his position and create the right circumstances for opening up the queenside with axb5 himself.

13...♗c8 14.b3

14...h5!

This powerful pawn break highlights the drawback of the premature g2-g4 push and was the solution to **Exercise 1**. Both 14...a5 15.a4! and 14...♘d7 15.a4! fail to attack White's weakest spot and force Black to divide his attention between both sides of the board.

On move 8 the white queen has already moved three times but lured the black c-pawn to c4

15.♘e5 ♘xe5 16.dxe5 ♘d7

17.bxc4

There was no need to release the tension so early, because ...cxb3 will never really be a threat.

17.♘f3! hxg4 18.hxg4 would have led to Exercise 2 with the b-pawns still on the board. This is in White's favour, because he will be able to play ♘d4 with tempo, forcing Black to reckon with bxc4 all the time.

17...hxg4 18.hxg4 bxc4 19.♘f3

We have arrived at **Exercise 2**. The aim was to identify White's most vulnerable spot and exploit it.

19...f6

It is very tempting to open up the long diagonal for the bishop, but this pawn trade also improves the white pieces. Attacking the vulnerable e5-pawn with 19...♕b6 20.♖b1 ♕e6 wasn't the right solution either, because White can simply repel the queen with 21.♘d4.

Instead, Black should have focused on the poorly protected g4-pawn and the vulnerable light squares in his opponent's camp with 19...♘c5! 20.♘d4 ♕d7!.

ANALYSIS DIAGRAM

Black is threatening to launch a double attack on White's queen and e-pawn with 21...♘d3!, with 22.♗xd3 due to be refuted by 22...♕xg4+!. White should defend his light squares with the passive 21.♕d1, but this will make him ill-equipped if Black opens up the position with 21...f6! after all.

20.exf6 ♖xf6 21.♖d1

21...♕e8 There was no need to give up the d5-pawn so easily. 21...♘b6 would have kept the game level.

22.♖xd5 ♗b7

Black attacks the rook and is probably hoping for a quick ...e7-e5 to exploit the poorly placed white minor pieces on the f-file.

23.♗xc4

This move worked out very well in the game, but was not the correct answer to **Exercise 3**. 23.♖d1 is not very impressive either, as it only leads to an unclear position after 23...♘b6. Instead, White should have kept his rook on the fifth rank with 23.♖a5!.

ANALYSIS DIAGRAM

The rook is very safe on the fifth rank, where it controls the important e5-square. After 23...♕c8, Black is a pawn down and is stuck with several vulnerable pawns requiring protection. In the meantime, White can slowly build up a kingside attack, e.g.

Black is a pawn down and is stuck with several vulnerable pawns requiring protection. In the meantime, White can slowly build up a kingside attack

with 24.♕f1 ♘b6 25.♕h3!, followed by ♘g5.

23...♔f8

This passive move fails to put White to the test. Black should have focused on the undefended f3-knight to force his opponent into an unclear exchange sacrifice with 23...e6! 24.♖xd7.

24.♘g5! Well played! Directing the knight towards the vulnerable black king was the solution to **Exercise 4**. White had to be precise, since he could have run into a counterattack after both 24.g5 ♖xf4! 25.exf4 ♘b6, and 24.♕d1 ♘b6! 25.♖d4 ♘xc4 26.♖xc4 ♗xf3 27.♕xf3 g5.
24...e5 25.♘h7+ ♚e7 26.♕a3+ ♚d8

White has successfully driven the enemy king towards the centre and has many winning continuations available. He chooses the most forcing one.
27.♖xd7+ ♕xd7 28.♘xf6 ♗xf6 29.♕f8+ ♚c7 30.♕c5+ ♚d8

31.♕f8+ ♚c7 32.♕xf6 ♕xg4+ 33.♗g3 ♕xc4

34.♕xe5+
34.♗xe5+ would have been more practical, since it does not allow the king to cross the sixth rank so easily. White wins by force after 34...♚c8 35.♕f8+ ♚d7 36.♖d1+ ♚c6 37.♕d6+ ♚b5 38.♖b1+ ♚a5 39.♕a3+ ♕a4 40.♗c7+ ♚a6 41.♕xa4 mate.
34...♚b6 35.♕d6+ ♗c6

36.♕c7+ The queen was already well-placed on d6 and it would have been more effective to activate the white rook with 36.♖b1+ ♚a6 37.♖b3. White will have to be careful after the text move, since positions with opposite-coloured bishops are very tricky, and his own king could easily become a target as well.
36...♚a6 37.♕e5

Exposing your opponent's Achilles' heel and developing the right tools to attack often pays dividends

White should have focused on his own weaknesses instead. Blocking the long diagonal with 37.f3! was the only way to preserve an advantage.
37...♖d8! 38.♕e7 ♖h8

Black is on his way to exposing White's Achilles' heel.
39.♕a3+ The tables will turn quickly after this check. Shutting out the black bishop with 39.f3 (or 39.e4) was again required.
39...♚b7 40.♕b2+ ♚a8

White reached move 40, only to find out that a well-deserved victory had completely slipped through his fingers. Chess can be a cruel game...
41.f3 ♗xf3 42.♚f2 ♗b7 43.♖b1 ♕f7+ 44.♚e1 ♖h1+ 45.♚d2 ♕d5+ 46.♚e2 ♕g2+ 47.♚f2 ♕f3+ 48.♚d3 ♗e4+
White resigned.

Conclusion
Exposing your opponent's Achilles' heel and developing the right tools to attack often pays dividends. White played a good game, but allowed the enemy king to escape, after which his own weakness turned out to be fatal. ∎

MAXIMize your Tactics Solutions

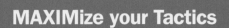

1. Gritsayeva-Nasyrova
Cheboksary 2021

Black played 36...♖d8 and the game eventually ended in a draw. What she missed was the stunning **36...♕xc2+! 37.♕xc2 ♗d4** mate.

2. R.Vasquez-Ter Sahakyan
Titled Arena 2021

Black's faraway pieces manage to get at White's king quickly: **40...♗g1+! 41.♔h3** If 41.♔xg1 ♘e2+, winning the queen. **41...♕h1** mate.

3. L.Nozdrachev-Rathanvel
Titled Tuesday 2021

26.♕xf8+! ♔xf8 27.♖d8+ Black resigned, as on 27...♔e7 the discovered double check 28.♗g5 protects the rook and mates.

4. Basso-Froewis
Mitropa Online Cup 2021

28...♕g2+! No, White didn't blunder mate in one, but this queen sacrifice allows Black to create a well-known pattern: 29.♘xg2 ♘f3+ 30.♔h1 ♖xh2 mate. White resigned.

5. Barsegyan-Cuenca
Barcelona 2021

24...♖xd6! Eliminating the strong white knight. **25.exd6 ♕xe2 26.♗xe2** And White resigned, as after 26...c5+ he is checkmated.

6. Korkmaz-Gunina
Titled Tuesday 2021

After **20...♖xf4!** White chose to go on a piece down (21.♗h3 ♖f2) and duly lost. Black's point was **21.♗xf4 ♘xd3+ 22.cxd3 ♗xf4+**, winning the queen.

7. Andreikin-Can
Sochi World Cup 2021

21.♗xe5 fxe5 Now that Black's control of the g6-square is less firm and the f-file is open, it's time to strike: **22.♘g6+! ♔g8** The main line goes 22...hxg6 23.♕h3+ ♔g8 24.♖xf8+ ♖xf8 25.♕xd7 with huge material gains. **23.♘xf8** And Black resigned two moves later.

8. Rogic-Lagarde
Mitropa Online Cup 2021

The white king's situation is fraught with danger, but the black rook is attacked and in case of 25...♖d2 White will continue to bother it by 26.♘b1. However, after **25...♘d1!** he had to resign, in view of 26.♘xe2 ♖f1 mate, or 26.♖xd1 ♖g2 mate, or 26.♘g3 ♖e1+, mating.

9. Raahul-Delchev
Arandjelovac 2021

After **30.♗xd6! ♖xd6** Black resigned before 31.♖a2 was executed. 30...cxd6 fails to the same rook swing: 31.♕xb6+ ♔c8 32.♕c6+ ♔b8 33.♖a2, mating. 30...♕xd2 doesn't save either because of 31.♕xb6+ ♔a8 32.♕c6+ ♔a7 33.♕xc7+ ♔a8 34.♕xd8+ ♔b7 35.♕b8 mate.

From the horse's mouth

Mark Taimanov's candid account of his traumatic 6-0 loss to Bobby Fischer, and Nigel Short's equally personal and revealing guide to winning tournaments were two of the books that **MATTHEW SADLER** devoured during his summer holidays.

With a frenetic period at work behind me, I decided on a complete change of scenery for my holidays. Configuring my out-of-office assistant with the standard message ('Don't try to call me, you'll never find me anyway...') I slammed the screen of my work laptop shut, stood up from my desk with an exhilarating sense of freedom... and moved 50 cm to the right to my home laptop! With the British government randomly changing advice on allowed holiday destinations on a daily basis, I didn't fancy the stress of a foreign holiday; and with the weather having decided that Britain is now a tropical island and should therefore receive a mix of torrential rain and baking sunshine (though mostly torrential rain), a British vacation seemed a touch risky.

It wasn't so bad in fact. I'd spent a couple of months co-developing the opening book for the TCEC engine championship Superfinal (a 100-game match between Stockfish and Leela, convincingly won by Stockfish 56-44), so it was nice to follow those games intensely as well as stream on them. And I also got to attend my first in-person chess event for a year and a half with the amazing ChessFest in Central London. Chess taking over Trafalgar Square was not a sight I had ever expected to see and yet there it was on a really huge scale – huge plaudits to Malcolm Pein and the Chess in Schools charity for organising it! And, of course, I also got to read some books!

Far-reaching consequences

I was a victim of Bobby Fischer by Mark Taimanov (Quality Chess) has an unusual genesis. Taimanov submitted the manuscript for publication in 1992, and this retrospective on his games with the great Bobby Fischer – and in particular the famous match in Vancouver in 1971 which he lost 6-0 – was also a lament on the disappearance of the great American from the chess world. Not for the first time, Bobby threw Taimanov's plans into confusion by returning to chess for his second match with Spassky! The Russian edition was published anyway in 1993 and now we finally have an English edition translated by Douglas Griffin.

Taimanov was adamant that the flow of his text should not be altered by computer analysis so Quality Chess has taken an imaginative approach to providing a modern perspective on Taimanov's games and thoughts which I think works beautifully. Firstly, some discreet footnotes point readers to a chapter compiled by the translator with analysis notes from other human commentators. Secondly, twelve critical positions from the match (and an additional game of Taimanov's) were given to three young grandmasters (Sam Shankland, Jeffery Xiong and Awonder Liang) who were asked to analyse them (without an engine!) and provide their conclusions, which Jacob Aagaard summarised and corrected where appropriate. It's a lovely idea and also adds a training element that wasn't present in the original book! There's also a short biography of Taimanov, an interview and some additional material and games to round off the book.

As to Taimanov's text, I really loved it! There's something quite moving about the enthusiasm and joy with which Taimanov recounts an experience that – from the score point of view – was an absolute low-point in his career, with far-reaching and deeply negative personal consequences, not only for his chess career but also for his alternate career as a concert pianist (a 'true' Soviet grandmaster could not possibly lose 6-0 to an American and so had to be punished). Also – very much like Nigel Short's *Winning* which I review later – it's really interesting to live games through the player's eyes, understanding how he prepared, what he saw, and how his moods varied within the context of an entire event. How his moods varied you might ask – he lost 6-0! However, the crux is that the match was considerably closer than the score could ever make you imagine. Fischer had to exert himself mightily in every game and was in severe trouble in several of the games. However, Fischer displayed not only resolute defensive ability, he managed to set his opponent nerve-wracking problems even while worse. He did this partly through consistently active defence – which meant that even in a clearly better position, Taimanov only seemed one misstep away from defeat (very much like the experience of playing against an engine!) – and also (it seems to me) by playing – perhaps intuitively, perhaps just as a result of relentlessly playing optimal moves – on Taimanov's irrepressibly optimistic character by giving him opportunities to go wrong at every phase of the game.

This last thought struck me when considering Taimanov's catastrophic blunder in the 5th game.

Mark Taimanov
Bobby Fischer
Vancouver 1971 (Candidates match-5)

position after 44.♖f1

44...♕e4 Taimanov: 'I recall that in analysis we had in the main examined the reply 44...♕e5, leading after the exchange of queens to a slightly worse endgame for Black. The move

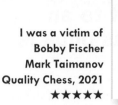
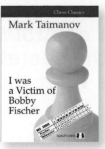

I was a victim of Bobby Fischer
Mark Taimanov
Quality Chess, 2021
★★★★★

Eight Good Men
Dorian Rogozenco
Elk and Ruby, 2021
★★★★☆

actually played by Fischer was unanimously rejected, according to the general opinion that it was inexpedient for him to give up the f6-pawn.'
45.♕c7+ ♔h6

Taimanov: 'Here I thought for a few minutes – confused by the thought: why had Fischer all the same gone in for the sacrifice of the pawn? And then I found an explanation – Fischer does not like passive defence and therefore preferred 44...♕e4 to the move 44...♕e5. Now after 46.♖xf6 he replies 46...♖a2 and I would have to exchange queens with 47.♕f4+ ♕xf4 48.♖xf4 and his rook takes up an active position on c2 which guarantees Fischer the draw. Well alright, I decided, it will at least be a moral victory – an extra pawn.
'The following took place in a matter of seconds.'
46.♖xf6 ♕d4+ 47.♖f2 ♖a1+ 0-1.

'And once again I resigned. Even now twenty years later I feel the sensation of bitterness, injustice and the cruelty of fate that I experienced back then. We both left the stage silently.'

Even 4-0 down, Taimanov was still thinking only about being better – an amazingly positive attitude, but one that blinded him to a simple trap.

In summary, a really wonderful book and a beautiful testimony both to the astonishing Bobby Fischer and to the strange but wonderful fact that our most devastating losses can sometimes become our most cherished memories. 5 stars.

■ ■ ■

Eight Good Men by Dorian Rogozenco (Elk and Ruby) is an account of (perhaps?) the longest over-the-board chess tournament ever played: the 2020-2021 Candidates tournament that started in March 2020 and ended in April 2021! Every game is extensively annotated, three quarters by Dorian Rogozenco, with one game each round annotated by a special guest. The guests are... pretty good: Kasparov, Ponomariov, Kasimdzhanov, Gelfand, Harikrishna, Nielsen, to name but a few!

The Candidates is traditionally one of my favourite tournaments – I have wonderful memories of watching

Even in a clearly better position, Taimanov only seemed one misstep away from defeat (very much like the experience of playing against an engine!)

Keeping yourself under control throughout the highs and lows is the secret to an elite career and that is what this book is all about

the 2013 London Candidates (all-time greatest in my opinion) and the 2018 Berlin Candidates in person – but this one somehow got lost in the sands of time for me. I was very keen on the first half but never got into the restart. For that reason, it was really nice to have a book bringing all the games seamlessly together.

Perhaps the most striking thing when you see all the games in one place is how hard-fought they were and how unbelievably good the elite players are nowadays. In an era when engines give instant verdicts over players' moves (which we didn't have in my day, thank goodness) and where the top players are playing so much at all types of time controls (also quite different to my day) it's easy to become a little jaded and dismissive of top human chess. But looking at the quality of chess that players produce when they play at long time-controls for an important goal, you can't help but feel enormous respect.

As you can tell, I greatly enjoyed this book. Rogozenco's comments are consistently excellent and the different guest annotators spice up the material nicely. A really good book – 4 stars!

■ ■ ■

Perhaps the funniest part of *Winning* by Nigel Short (Quality Chess) is the very start of Peter Svidler's introduction: 'When Nigel told me, last year, that he was writing a book, my reaction was a combination of "oh noooo" and "I'm pre-ordering". Those who are familiar with Nigel's somewhat combative takes on all things chess-related will probably recognise my emotions' ... which is indeed a perfect summary of *my* feelings when Nigel told me about his plans!

This book is structured in an

extremely original way – I can't think of another book like it – and provides some truly unique insights. Rather than write a collection of his best games, Nigel elected to write a collection of his best tournaments. Essentially this is an account of events where the war was won – tournament victory was achieved – but not every battle went according to plan!

Whenever players win a tournament, they are always asked to annotate their best games. The reader gets the impression that all of the winner's games were played to this standard, and often (I speak from experience) the winner himself also starts to look back on the tournament in the same way, the glow of victory smoothing over the memory of rough moments with the feeling that victory was inevitable and deserved.

But as any experienced player knows, no victory against a strong field is ever as easy as the best games. There are also missed opportunities against players you expected to beat, there are the short draws that ruined your momentum, there are miserable games in which you were in trouble but hung on to save a crucial half point. Keeping yourself under control throughout the highs and lows is the secret to an elite career and that is what this book is all about.

A more realistic image

Nigel takes us through each round of eight of his tournament victories covering a time period of just under 30 years, annotating each game in detail. Interestingly – now aided by computer assistance – he also corrects mistakes that he made in his earlier annotations to some of these games, which demonstrates the striking truth that your impressions of your

games in the pre-computer age often strongly differed from reality!

I wish I'd had a book like this when I was a promising young player. I think it would have given me a more realistic image of the natural course of a tournament, and perhaps less emotional when the inevitable bad game (or bad move) reared its head.

The annotations to Nigel's win against the Spanish grandmaster Jordi Magem are quite typical. Some tournament context, some psychological musings, not too many complex variations and some good moves!

Nigel Short
Jordi Magem
Pamplona 1999
Sicilian Defence, Taimanov Variation

'Ignorance is bliss, they say, so thankfully I didn't lose any sleep over my unexpected missed opportunity against Judit [Nigel only discovered it when preparing this book!]. Jordi Magem Badals is a respectable GM but if you are hoping to win tournaments, you have to win your points somewhere. In this strong round-robin, he seemed as good a target as any. Especially with the white pieces. There was no reason to go crazy – just sensibly play and hope to press him. A draw would only be a mild disappointment.'

1.e4 c5 2.♘c3 e6 3.♘f3 ♘c6 4.d4 cxd4 5.♘xd4 ♕c7 6.♗e2 a6 7.0-0 ♘f6 8.♔h1 ♘xd4 9.♕xd4 ♗c5 10.♕d3 b5 11.f4 ♗b7 12.♗f3 h5

13.♗d2

Winning
Nigel Short
Quality Chess, 2021
★★★★★

'If you outrate your opponent, let him play his own moves! The main line goes 13.e5 ♘g4 14.♗xb7 ♕xb7 15.♘e4. This is a terribly well-chewed piece of meat. This would be fine if it offered an objective advantage. But I wasn't sure. Mediocre practical results bear out my pessimism.'

13...♘g4 14.♕e2 g6

'On the very few occasions this position has been reached, some peculiar moves have been ventured. 14...♗d4?! is wafting around and the exceedingly optimistic 14...g5? was ventured by Ruth Sheldon, former gold-medallist at the 1998 Girls World Under 18 Championship, and now a lecturer in Religion and Social Science at King's College London. Both these moves are well met by 15.e5!. In the latter case, probably decisively. The direct 14...b4 was the way to go.

15.♖ac1

'I am not sure that this qualifies as one of those "mysterious rook moves" of which Nimzowitsch was so fond. It protects the c-pawn and places the tower indirectly opposite the queen which can never be a bad idea. My basic plan was to maintain the complexity and to ask Black what he wanted to do with his king? Indeed he never managed to adequately answer that question.'

15...♖c8 16.a3

'To discourage the disruptive ...b4.'

16...f5 17.h3 'Of course there is no threat to take the knight at the moment, but there may be.'

17...♔f7 'Magem chooses the safest square for his monarch, as well as connecting the rooks.'

18.♖cd1 ♕b6

'People often feel psychological and physiological discomfort when the tension is maintained for a sizable length of time, and thus try to resolve it to their detriment. Indeed, Garry Kimovich, no less, once told me that I was unable to withstand tension. Never having attended the Botvinnik School, this came as an alien concept, but I thought about it and concluded, some years later, that he might have a point. Here Magem tries to force the pace by making the threat of a fork. But it is easily rebuffed effectively.'

19.♗e1 ♖c7 20.exf5

'My turn to release the tension. 20.♖d3, avoiding the fork on e3, was better.'

20...gxf5 21.♗xb7 ♕xb7 22.♖f3 ♘f6 23.♗h4 ♘e4

'Remember what I said about forcing matters! This is far too loose. 23...♗e7 maintains the balance. The black king is slightly exposed, but Black has the better pawn structure.'

24.♘xe4 ♕xe4

'After 24...fxe4 25.♖g3 the attack is already unstoppable.'

25.♕d2

'White is never going to exchange queens! Instead she will infiltrate

on the dark squares, the g-file, the centre – wherever to deliver checkmate. The attack can no longer be resisted.'

25...♖hc8

' 25...♖g8 would have made it harder, but no more: 26.♖c3 ♕b7 27.♕e2 wins by switching the attack to the kingside.'

26.♖e1 ♕c6 27.♖g3

'The h-pawn is a juicy target.'

27...♕d6 28.♖d3 ♕c6 29.♕e2 ♖h8 30.♕e5

'The final assault begins.'

30...♖g8

'30...♖h6 31.♗g5 ♖g6 32.♕h8 would not have helped.'

31.♕f6+ ♔e8 32.♗g5

'Black is paralysed. That, and the unstoppable threat of ♕xf5 renders his position utterly hopeless.'

I enjoyed this book greatly. There are inevitably a few places where you raise your eyebrows and think 'Nigel, did this really need to be included...?' However, the opportunity to hear the thoughts of a great player on how to win across 8 tournaments is something quite unique and worthy of 5 stars!

■ ■ ■

Brits play the London

I also spent quite a bit of time during my holiday commentating together with Natasha Regan on the British Online Championships. It was fun to do, though I did wonder at times whether I'd stumbled into a London System thematic tournament. I threw my arms up in despair when even top-seed Michael Adams joined in the fun! So I guess that *The London System in 12 Practical Lessons* by Oscar de Prado (New In Chess) would be an excellent birthday present for most of the English chess players!

It follows on from the same author's *The Agile London System* which focused on the theory of the opening. This book is more practical in nature, focusing on thematic and practical aspects of the London System. We have chapters on London System move-orders (dealing with the fiends who might try and avoid it!), the attack on the b2-pawn, the early exchange of the f4-bishop (dealing with the resulting pawn structures after the exchange of the dark-squared bishop on f4 or g3), quick h4 ideas and typical London System queen manoeuvres. There are also a few theoretical chapters towards the end dealing with the develop-ments since the previous book was published as well as a response to the book *Fighting the London System* by Kiril Georgiev, published a year after De Prado's first book!

Let's take a look at one theme which will give you a good idea of the type of content in the book: Typical queen manoeuvres in the London System.

'The white queen also plays an important role in the London System. In addition to coming out to b3, as we've seen in the variations where there is play on the queenside, espe-cially when Black plays ...♗f5 and leaves b7 weak, the queen also has other squares that it frequently uses. One of White's objectives is to attack the enemy king and for this the queen often takes the route f3-h3 to attack h7, unless it's able to go to h5 immediately.

'We can also encounter a plan involving ♕b1, with the idea of provoking weaknesses in Black's castled position and then returning (via d1-f3) to the kingside. We've already seen this plan mentioned in one game and it also arises in the Torre Attack, among other openings.

The London System in 12 Practical Lessons
Oscar de Prado
New In Chess, 2021
★★★★☆

The queen can also play on the queenside, not only on b3, but also on a3, a4 or a5, to put pressure on Black's queenside weaknesses.

Magnus Carlsen
Vishy Anand
Doha World Blitz 2016 (20)
London System

1.d4 ♘f6 2.♗f4 d5 3.e3 c5 4.c3 ♘c6 5.♘d2 e6 6.♘gf3 ♗d6 7.♗g3 0-0 8.♗b5 a6
'We have already seen this position in the previous lesson. This move is bad, since White is intending to exchange on c6 anyway, so Black loses a tempo, as well as weakening his queenside pawns.
9.♗xc6 bxc6 10.♕a4

'A good queen move. In this game, the plan will be to attack Black's weaknesses on the queenside. From

This book will prove invaluable to the hordes of London System addicts out there

a4, the queen takes aim at c6 and in particular it envisages moving to a3 from where it will attack c5.
10...♖b8 11.♕a3 ♗xg3 12.hxg3 cxd4 13.cxd4 a5 14.0-0 ♕b6 15.b3 ♗a6 16.♖fc1
'Black is worse. The c6-pawn is weak, and so is the one on a5. It's very important that Black is unable to free his position. Nevertheless, it's striking to observe how Anand's position collapses in just a few moves.
16...♘d7 17.♕d6

'Again the queen plays the major role. After this strong move, attacking both the c6-pawn and the knight, Black is in serious difficulties.
17...♕a7 18.♖xc6
'The game is decided: White already has an extra pawn and the better position, with absolute control of the c-file but now in addition White is winning more material, due to the simultaneous attack on a6 and d7.
18...♗b5 19.♖c7 ♖b7 20.♖ac1 a4 21.♖xb7 ♕xb7 22.♖c7 ♕b8 23.♖xd7 ♗xd7 24.♕xd7 1-0.
'A good model game illustrating some possible queen manoeuvres in the London. In this case the idea of ♕a4-a3 stood out, putting pressure on the queenside dark squares.'

I always like books organised along thematic lines and I think that this book will prove invaluable to the hordes of London System addicts out there, grouping together tech-niques in the opening, middlegame and endgame in a pleasantly readable manner. Last book of the holidays, feeling generous: 4 stars! ∎

Aimchess
Learn chess **your way**

Hi, we're Aimchess
We help chess players like you improve by using our fancy computers to give you simple insights on how to improve your rating, i.e. *you should work on your time management because you're behind on the clock for 70% of your moves.*

Then we make a weekly study plan for you where we create lessons using positions from your recent games (and some of our own fun ones as well).

If you'd like to try Aimchess, sign up at:
aimchess.com/try

For 30% off your 1st month of Premium use promo code:
newinchess30

Test your chess knowledge with these puzzles

A **Chose a better move**
White to play.

B **Practice your visualization**
White to move and win (to increase your challenge, don't use the board).

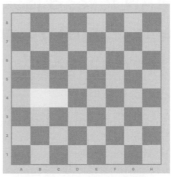

♙ a7   ♔ b6   ♜ b4   ♚ f8

C **Test your defensive chess**
Black to move.

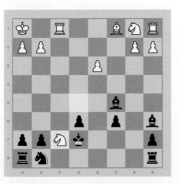

Jan Timman

Asian prodigies on the rise

With 206 participants and many hundreds of games, the World Cup in Sochi produced an abundance of stories of success and failure. **JAN TIMMAN** takes a look at the remarkable achievements of three youngsters whose ambitions know no bounds.

It was a striking statistic that in the quarter final of the World Cup in Sochi, Magnus Carlsen was the only Top-10 player left. All other favourites had been eliminated in the earlier stages. Curiously enough, the players that had been instrumental in removing them had also succumbed during the long race. Who were the giant-killers? Interestingly, they were mainly representatives from the former Soviet republics. Thirty-two-year-old Rinat Jumabaev from Kazakhstan defeated Fabiano Caruana early on. I was also impressed by two junior players from Uzbekistan. For a long time, Rustam Kasimdzhanov had been their only top player, but this seems to be changing.

Sixteen-year-old Nodirbek Abdusattorov eliminated Anish Giri, while 15-year-old Javokhir Sindarov managed to get the better of another phenomenal junior player, Alireza Firouzja.

Abdusattorov is the prototype of a *Wunderkind*. At nine years of age, he beat two grandmasters in his native Tashkent, and two years later, he scored his first grandmaster result. That was unheard of, but in the end he failed to become the youngest GM of all time, lacking the possibilities and backing to play more tournaments. Abdusattarov, meanwhile, has developed further, and his rating is now well over 2600. In Sochi, he first defeated 21-year-old Indian GM Chithambaram Aravindh.

Chithambaram Aravindh
Nodirbek Abdusattorov
Sochi World Cup 2021 (2.2)
Semi-Tarrasch Defence

1.d4 d5 2.c4 e6 3.♘c3 ♘f6 4.cxd5 ♘xd5 5.e4 ♘xc3 6.bxc3
c5 7.♘f3 cxd4 8.cxd4 ♗b4+ 9.♗d2 ♗xd2+ 10.♕xd2 0-0 11.♗c4 ♘d7 12.0-0 b6 13.♖fe1 ♗b7 14.♖ad1 ♖c8 15.♗b3 h6

This move was frequently played by Rakhmanov in the past. Abdusattorov had played it several times before this year, so Aravindh must have been prepared for it. Alternatives are 15...♘f6, as in the famous game Keres-Fine, Ostend 1937, and 15...♖e8.

16.♖e3 A logical way to reinforce the position.

16...♘f6

This direct approach is Black's best way to generate sufficient counterplay. Abdusattorov had played 16...♖e8 in an online game against Khademalsharieh, but this move allows White to grab the advantage with 17.♕e2 ♘f6 18.h3.

17.d5 exd5 18.♕e1

18.exd5 is critical, as in Eljanov-Keymer, Douglas 2019, in which there followed 18...♕d6 19.♘h4 ♖fe8 20.♘f5 ♕d7, and now White has the following options:

– 21.♖f3 Eljanov's choice. After 21...♗xd5 22.♘xh6+ ♔f8 the position was equal.

– 21.♘xh6+ gxh6 22.♖g3+ ♔h7 23.♗c2+ ♖xc2 24.♕xc2+ ♔h8 25.♕c1 ♔h7 26.♖h3 was seen in Lazavik-Keymer, a blitz game earlier this year. Black could have preserved the balance here with 26...h5 (or 26...♘g4).

Two months earlier, Lazavik had played 18.e5 against Abdusattorov. After 18...♘e4 19.♕e1 ♕e7 20.♘d4 ♕h4 Abdusattorov had absolutely no problems. Nor did the text cause him any trouble.

18...♖e8 19.e5 ♘g4 20.♖e2 ♗a6 21.♖xd5 The e2-rook had no good squares. After 21.♖ed2 ♘f6 Black would be fine.

21...♕xd5!
A sharply calculated transaction. Black temporarily sacrifices a piece.
22.♗xd5 ♗xe2 23.♕xe2 ♖c1+ 24.♘e1 ♘xe5

The point of Black's play is becoming clear. White cannot avoid losing his knight.

25.♔h1 The alternative 25.♔f1 was no better. Black still regains the piece: 25...♔f8 26.g3 ♘c4.
25...♔f8 26.h3

This is why White played his king to h1. He wants it to go to h2, but it isn't clear whether it will be better positioned there.

26...♘c4 27.♕f3 ♖cxe1+ 28.♔h2 ♘e5 29.♕a3+ ♖e7 30.f4 ♖e3 A teasing move that has no effect on the assessment of the position: the

Abdusattorov is the prototype of a Wunderkind

Nodirbek Abdusattorov (16) caused one of the biggest upsets in the World Cup as he eliminated one of the top seeds, Anish Giri.

chances are equal, although Black has the more pleasant game.
31.♕c1 ♘g6 32.♕c8+ ♖e8 33.♕c7 33.♕f5 was also possible. After 33...♖3e7 34.♗xf7 ♖xf7 35.♕xg6 ♖f6 36.♕d3 it's beginning to look like a draw.
33...♖3e7 34.♕d6 ♘h4 35.♗c6 An inaccuracy that allows Black to develop a dangerous initiative. With 35.g4!, White could just have preserved the balance, taking away square f5 from the black knight. It seems problematic to compromise the shield around the king, but there's no way for Black to exploit this. After 35...♘g8 36.f5 ♖e3 37.♕d7 the position is equal.

35...♘f5! 36.♕d3 ♖c8 37.♗e4 ♘e3! The point of the 35th move.

38.f5 After this second inaccuracy White is lost. His only chance was 38.♕d6, although even then Black stays firmly in control with 38...♘f1+ 39.♔g1 ♘g3 40.♗d3 ♘h5! – the knight is en route to f6.

38...♘f1+ 39.♔g1 ♘g3 The knight is indefatigable. In the end, Black forces a swap of the minor pieces.

40.♕xg3 ♖xe4 41.♕d6+ ♔g8 42.♕d7 ♖a8

The most systematic move. Black is in no hurry. **43.♕b7 ♖ee8 44.a4 f6 45.♔h2 a5 46.♕xb6 ♖e5 47.g4 ♖c8 48.♕b3+ ♔h7 49.♔g3 ♖ec5 50.♔h4 ♖c3**

Slowly but surely, White is forced back. **51.♕e6 ♖d8 52.♕f7 ♖e3 53.♕b7 ♖dd3 54.♕g2 ♖a3 55.♕h1 ♖f3 56.♕g2 ♖ad3 57.♕h1 g5+ 58.fxg6+ ♔xg6 59.♕g2 ♖xh3+** White resigned.

Impressive knight manoeuvres

In the next round, the Uzbek star had to square up to Anish Giri. In the classical games there was little between them. He managed to create a slight plus as White, hanging on to it till deep in the endgame. In the

second game, Abdusattorov held his own remarkably easily. He had opted for the French, which apparently took Giri by surprise, because he failed to create any opening advantage.

In the first tie-break game, Giri again failed to make a dent in the French.

Anish Giri
Nodirbek Abdusattorov
Sochi World Cup 2021 (3.3)

position after 31...f5

32.g4 An unjustified winning attempt in an equal position. The black knight will take a leading part now. Giri should have been warned after Abdusattorov's win over Aravindh! After 32.f3 ♘c3 33.♖e6 a draw is inevitable, e.g. 33...♖d2 34.♘e5 ♖d1+ 35.♔f2 ♖d2+.

32...♘g5! A nasty little move for White. **33.♔g2 fxg4 34.♔g3 ♘f3** 34...h5 would probably have been stronger, e.g. 35.♖e5 ♖d2 36.♘f4 ♘f7 37.♖e8+ ♔h7 38.♘xh5 ♖b2, and it's not certain that White will be able to hold.

35.♖e7 ♖d2 36.♘f4 d3

37.♖e3? Overlooking a finesse.

With 37.♔xg4 ♖xf2 38.♘xd3 ♘xh2+ 39.♔h4 White would have kept the game within drawing margins.

37...h5! 38.♘xh5 ♖d1 39.♔xg4 ♘xh2+ 40.♔f4 d2 41.♖d3 ♘f1! As in the game against Aravindh, the black knight assumes the leading part. White resigned, because he'll be unable to stop the d-pawn from queening.

In the second rapid game, Giri got a winning position, but was unable to convert his advantage: the young Uzbek was through. The confrontation with Giri must have cost Abdusattorov a great deal of energy. To the disappointment of his many fans, he went under against Vasif Durarbayli in the next round.

Daredevil

While Abdusattorov seems to be developing into a mainly strategical player, Javokhir Sindarov's style more resembles that of a daredevil. He plays sharp lines, and is not afraid of complications. His clash with Firouzja was interesting in every respect. For me, there was an additional juicy detail: two years earlier, I had some close encounters with the two young stars in Hoogeveen. Like me, they were staying in the Spaarbanckhoeve hotel, both accompanied by their fathers. On that occasion, Firouzja defeated the Peruvian GM Cori 4½-1½. Sindarov also gave a good account of himself by nearly winning the open tournament. He was already a grandmaster then, and he has developed further during those two years. He nearly eliminated Firouzja in the classical games already.

After a solid draw as Black, he was completely winning in his game as White.

Javokhir Sindarov
Alireza Firouzja
Sochi World Cup 2021 (2.2)
Sicilian Defence, Najdorf Variation

1.e4 c5 2.♘c3 d6 3.♘f3 ♘f6 4.d4 cxd4 5.♘xd4 a6 6.h3 e6 7.g4 ♗e7 8.♗g2 ♘fd7 9.♗e3 ♘c6 10.h4

The usual move is 10.♕e2 to prepare castling queenside. The text is sharper, and cannot have come as a surprise for Firouzja, since Sindarov had already played this before.

10...0-0

In Sindarov-Okkes, Hoogeveen 2019, Black played 10...♘de5. There followed 11.g5 ♗d7 12.♘xc6 bxc6 13.b3, and now Black should have gone 13...h5. It is important to enable the knight to sortie to g4.

Firouzja decides to avoid a direct confrontation in the centre and to wait till White has developed his queen to e2.

11.g5 ♘de5 12.♕e2 ♗d7 13.f4 ♘xd4 14.♗xd4 ♘c6 15.♗e3 ♘a5 16.0-0-0 ♖c8 17.♗d4

17...♘c4

Probably stronger than the alternative 17...b5. After 18.♕f2 ♘c4 19.f5 Black would be in trouble, as witness:
– 19...b4 20.f6 bxc3 21.♗xc3 e5 22.♗h3 (or 22.fxe7 first), and White is better;
– 19...e5 20.♘d5 exd4 21.f6 ♖e8 22.fxe7 ♕a5 23.♔b1 ♗e6 24.♖xd4 ♗xd5 25.♖xd5 ♖xe7 26.c3, and here, too, White has a strategic plus.

18.f5

Sindarov plays sharp lines, and is not afraid of complications

18...e5

This is a concession with serious consequences. With the razor-sharp 18...♕a5!, Black could have maintained the balance, the idea being to continue with 19...e5 only after 19.f6. After 20.fxe7 ♖fe8 White has no advantage, e.g. 21.♕f2 (not 21.♗f2, in view of 21...♕b4) 21...♗e6! 22.♗f1 ♘xb2 23.♔xb2 ♕b4+ 24.♔c1 exd4 25.♘d5 ♗xd5 26.exd5 ♕a3+, and a draw by perpetual check.

19.♗f2 ♕a5 20.♖d5!

Square d5 is usually reserved for the white knight in the Sicilian. In this position, Black's play is completely disrupted by the centralized rook.

20...♕b4

Consistent; but 20...b5 would have given him better chances of survival.

Javokir Sindarov (15) showed great determination. The young Uzbek came close to knocking out Alireza Firouzja in the classical part, and then struck in the final tiebreak game.

A possible continuation is: 21.♗e1 ♖c7 22.♔b1 ♖fc8 23.♖h3 g6 24.♕f1! ♕b6 25.♖d1!, and White remains better. Now the knight is poised to jump to d5.

21.♘d1 ♗d8 Black must bend over backwards to create some counter-play. 22.a3 would have been a simple but effective reply to 21...♕a4.

22.♕d3 Good enough, but the computer regards 22.c3, reducing the black's queen's elbow room even more, as stronger. After 22...♕a4 23.b3 ♕a3+ 24.♔b1 ♘b6 (after 24...♗b5 the simple 25.♖xb5 axb5 26.bxc4 wins) 25.♗xb6 ♗xb6 26.f6 ♗e6 27.♖d3 gxf6 28.♗h3, White is holding all the trumps. He gets to launch a decisive attack.

22...♗b6 23.♖f1
A plausible move, but one that allows for a hidden combination. With 23.♗xb6 ♕xb6 24.b3 ♘a3 25.♘e3 White could have kept complete control of the position.

23...♗xf2
Black misses his chance. With 23...♗a4! he could suddenly have created sufficient counter-chances. After the forced reply 24.a3 Black even has two tactical turns offering him sufficient counterplay:
– The elegant 24...♗e3+! is probably Black's best option. After 25.♗xe3 ♗xc2! 26.axb4 (stronger than 26.♕xc2, which is followed by 26...♘a3! 27.♗c5! ♘xc2 28.♗xb4 ♘xb4+ 29.♘c3 ♘xd5 30.exd5 ♖c4!, and Black is better) 26...♗xd3 27.♖xd3 ♘xe3+ 28.♘c3 ♘xg2 the position is equal.
– 24...♘xb2 25.axb4 (certainly

not 25.♘xb2? in view of 25...♗xc2) 25...♘xd3+ 26.♖xd3 ♗xc2+ 27.♔b1 ♖fc8!, and Black has just enough counterplay.

ANALYSIS DIAGRAM

A possible continuation is 28.♖c3 ♖2xc3 29.♘xc3 ♗xf2 30.♘xa4 ♗xh4 31.♘b6 ♖c6 32.♘d5 ♗xg5, with a strange position: Black has no fewer than four pawns for the piece, but in view of the strong blockade thrown up by White, he'll have to settle for a draw.
24.♖xf2 b5 25.♕b3 ♕e1 26.♕c3 ♕g1 27.♕f3 ♕e1 28.b3 ♗c6 29.♖d3 ♘a3

30.♖dd2 Adding another defensive move was unnecessary. With 30.f6! White could have launched a decisive attack. After 30...g6 31.h5 the open h-file will decide.
30...♖c7 31.♕e3 Forcing a queen swap, after which White keeps all his trumps.
31...♕xe3 32.♖xe3 b4 33.f6
In the end, White breaks through after all.
33...♘b5 34.fxg7 ♖d8 35.♘f5 ♘c3 Desperately looking for counterplay.
36.♖xd6 ♖xd6 37.♘xd6 ♔xg7 38.♖f6 ♘xa2+ 39.♔d2 ♘c3

40.♗f3 a5 41.♔e3
The straightforward 41.h5 would have led to a fairly easy victory. The text allows Black to create a measure of counterplay.

41...a4 Understandably, Black wants to open the queenside, but 41...♘b5 would have given him better chances of survival. With accurate play, White can preserve a decisive advantage: 42.♘f5+ ♔f8 43.h5 ♗d7 44.♗e2 ♘a3, and now 45.h6!. He needn't be afraid of the capture on c2, because after 45...♘xc2+ 46.♔d2 ♗xf5 47.exf5 ♘d4 48.g6 the white kingside pawns decide.
42.bxa4 ♗xa4 43.♗h5 ♖d7 44.♘f5+ ♔f8 45.♖b6 ♖d8 46.♖b7 ♗c2 47.♖xf7+ ♔g8 48.♘h6+ ♔h8 49.♖a7 ♗b3 50.♖b7
Not throwing away the win, but 50.♗f7! was more convincing. After 50...♗c2 51.♗c4 Black is completely bereft of defences.
50...♗c4

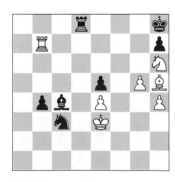

51.♖xb4
Sindarov played too fast here. With 51.♘f7+ ♗xf7 52.♗xf7 he could still have claimed the game, for example after 52...♖d4 53.h5 ♖xe4+

54.♔f3 ♖f4+ 55.♔g2 ♖g4+ 56.♔h3 ♖xg5 57.h6, and despite the reduced material, White has a mating attack.

51...♖d3+ 52.♔f2 ♘xe4+ 53.♔g1 The alternative 53.♔g2 eventually yielded nothing either: 53...♘d6 54.♖b8+ ♔g7 55.♖d8 ♗d5+! 56.♔g1 ♗e6, with the same consequences as in the game.

53...♘d6! Salvation. Sindarov must have overlooked this move.

54.♖b8+ ♔g7 55.♖d8 ♗e6 56.♗g4 ♖g3+ 57.♔f1 ♖xg4 58.♖xd6 ♖f4+ 59.♔g2 ♗c4

Now Black no longer has anything to fear, although Sindarov kept trying for a long time (½-½, 100).

A narrow escape for Firouzja. In the tie-breaks, Sindarov won the third game and progressed further. In the next round, he played against Jorge Cori, managing to beat the Peruvian convincingly as well.

After these victories Sindarov also ran out of steam, losing against Kacper Piorun in the next round. It is striking that both young Uzbek stars lost against 29-year-old grandmasters who had never really broken through to the top.

Not a single error
Sindarov and Abdusattorov are numbers four and six, respectively, on the list of youngest-ever grandmasters. Between them is the now 16-year-old Indian player Praggnanandhaa. I wrote about his achievements in rapid chess earlier this year. In Sochi, he showed that he has also grown very strong in classical chess, beating Sargissian 2-0. Their first game was a bit messy, but in the second one, the young Indian played very well, not making a single demonstrable error.

Gabriel Sargissian
Rameshbabu Praggnanandhaa
Sochi World Cup 2021 (2.2)
Queen's Gambit Accepted, Steinitz Variation

1.d4 d5 2.c4 dxc4 3.e3 ♘f6 4.♗xc4 e6 5.♘f3 c5 6.0-0 ♘c6 7.♘c3 a6 8.a3 b5 9.♗a2 ♗b7 10.d5

This advance is an old idea of Ufimtsev's, recently used successfully by Aronian.

10...exd5 11.♘xd5 ♘xd5 Probably the best option. In Aronian-Grischuk, Bucharest 2021, there followed 11...♗e7 12.e4 0-0 13.♗f4 c4 14.♖e1, and White was better.

12.♗xd5 ♗d6

13.e4 Two weeks earlier, this position had arisen in Shimanov-Shu-

valova, Cheboksary 2021, which continued: 13.b3 0-0 14.♗b2 ♕c7 15.♕d3 ♗e7 16.♘f5, and now 16...♖ad8 was the correct move (instead of the game move 16...♕d6). The point is revealed after 17.♘g5 ♗xg5 18.♕xg5 ♘d4!, and Black has equalized.

13...0-0 14.b4
With this pawn sacrifice, White tries to grab the initiative.

14...c4 Black could have accepted the pawn offer, because after 14...cxb4 15.axb4 ♗xb4 16.♗b2 ♗e7 White has nothing special. But the text is more principled, and strategically very sound.
15.♗b2 ♕c7 16.♕c2 ♗e7 17.♖ad1 ♖ad8 18.h3 ♖fe8 19.♘h2
White wants to transfer his knight to g4, intending to launch an attack. He will eventually get nowhere, but even after 19.♖d2, intending to double the rooks, Black will have sufficient counterplay. A good reaction would have been 19...a5.

19...♘b8 The correct plan: Black is going to force the centralized bishop to swap. The computer sees an even better way to execute this plan: 19...♗f8 20.♘g4 ♘e7!. After 21.♗xb7 ♕xb7 22.♘e3 ♕c6 Black is quite comfortable.

Rameshbabu Praggnanandhaa (16) has developed into a versatile all-round player. It was only in Round 4 that Maxime Vachier-Lagrave managed to stop the young Indian in Sochi.

20.♘g4 ♘d7 21.♕c3 More accurate was 21.♖fe1, with equal chances.
21...♘f6 22.♖fe1

22...h5!
A strong reaction, yielding Black an advantage. Praggnanandhaa has sharply calculated that the text won't weaken his position.
23.♘h6+
A desperate sacrifice. Sargissian must have realised that 23.♘e3 offered him scant winning chances. On the contrary; after 23...♗f8 24.♗xb7 ♕xb7 Black has a strategic plus in his protected passed pawn, e.g. 25.e5 (25.f3 can be met strongly by 25...h4!) 25...♘d5 26.♘xd5 ♖xd5 27.♕f3 ♖xd1 28.♕xd1 g6, with great prospects for Black.
23...gxh6 24.♗e3 h4

Keeping the rook away from g3. White doesn't have a real attack here, and Black's material superiority will decide the issue.
25.♖f3 ♖d6 26.g4 ♗d8
Black is slowly but surely freeing himself.
27.♔g2 ♕e7 28.♖f4 ♗xd5 29.♖xd5 ♖xd5 30.exd5 ♕d6 31.♕f3

31...♕xd5

The simplest option. Black liquidates to a totally winning endgame.

32.♗xf6 ♕xf3+ 33.♔xf3 ♗xf6 34.♖xf6 ♖e6 35.♖f5 ♖d6 36.♔e2 ♔g7 37.a4 bxa4 38.♖a5 ♖d3 39.♖xa4 ♖xh3 40.♖xa6 ♖b3 41.♖c6 h3 42.♖xc4 ♖b1

White resigned.

Young versus oldest

In the next round, Praggnanandhaa faced the oldest participant: Michal Krasenkow. The 57-year-old Polish grandmaster had just beaten Alekseenko in spectacular fashion. Praggnanandhaa managed to beat him convincingly as White. In the second game, he seemed to be en route for a second victory, but things didn't work out as planned.

Michal Krasenkow
Rameshbabu Praggnanandhaa
Sochi World Cup 2021 (3.2)
Queen's Gambit Accepted, Bogoljubow Defence

1.♘f3 d5 2.d4 ♘f6 3.c4 dxc4 4.♘c3 a6 5.e4 b5 6.e5 ♘d5 7.a4 e6 8.axb5 ♗b4 9.♕c2 ♘b6 10.♕e4

The start of an attacking plan that was deemed promising for a few

Praggnanandhaa showed that he has also grown very strong in classical chess

years, especially after Kasparov played it against me in Prague in 1998. Meanwhile, its sharp edges have worn off.

10...♕d5 11.♕g4 axb5 12.♖xa8 ♕xa8

13.♕xg7

This direct approach fails to yield an advantage. Crucial is 13.♗e2, as played by Kasparov. Black can then beat off the attack on the g-pawn in various ways, but 13...g6! is clearly the strongest. After 14.0-0 ♗xc3 15.bxc3 h6! White had insufficient compensation for the pawn in Gormally-Edouard, Birmingham 2016.

13...♗xc3+

Black can also play 13...♕a1 immediately, as in Komarov-Fominykh, Cairo 2001. In almost all cases, this makes no real difference. After 14.♕xh8+ ♔d7 15.♔d1 ♗xc3 Black should have forced a draw with 16.bxc3 ♕a4+ (instead of playing 16...♘d5) 17.♔d2 ♕a2+.

14.bxc3 ♕a1 15.♕xh8+ ♔d7 16.♗e2

A winning attempt that is justified in the sense that it doesn't upset the balance. From here on in,

however, the onus is on White to play accurately.

16...♕xc1+ 17.♗d1 ♕xc3+ 18.♘d2 ♘c6 19.♕xh7

19...♘xd4

The alternative 19...♘d5 is also fine, e.g. 20.h4 ♕xd4 21.♕e4 ♕b2 22.♘f3 ♕c3+ 23.♔f1 ♕c1 24.♕e1 c3 25.h5 c2 26.♗xc2 ♕xc2 27.h6 ♘de7 28.h7 ♘g6 29.h8♕ ♘xh8 30.♖xh8 b4, and the position is equal. The play remains sharp, though.

20.♕xf7+ White could also have played 20.h4 at once. After 20...♘d5 21.h5 ♘e3 22.♕xf7+ ♔c6 23.♕g6 ♘xd1 24.♔xd1 ♘f5 25.♕e8+ ♔b6 26.♘xc4+ bxc4 27.♕xc8 the position is equal.

20...♔c6

21.♕f4 A waste of tempo that could have proved fatal. He had two better moves.

First 21.♕g6, with the possible continuation 21...b4 22.h4 b3 23.♖h3 ♕c1 24.♕e4+ ♔c5 25.h5 b2 26.♖h4 ♘f5 27.♕c2!, and Black can't take the rook in view of a family check on b3. White escapes.

21.h4 is also possible, e.g. 21...b4 22.♖h3 ♕c1 23.♕g6 b3 24.♕e4+

♔c5 25.h5, and the game reverts to the previous variation.
21...♘d5 22.♕e4

At 57, Michal Krasenkow was one of the oldest participants in Sochi, but that did not stop the veteran from showing some spectacular chess.

22...♔c5 Even more convincing was 22...♔b6. After 23.h4 ♘b4 24.♖h3 ♘d3+ White can abandon all hope.
23.h4 ♗b7
Winning was 23...♘b4!, only developing the bishop with 25...♗b7 after 24.♕e3 ♘d3+ 25.♔f1. Black's minor pieces are incredibly strong.
24.h5 ♘b4 25.0-0!

Here the drawback of Black's 22nd move is revealed: he cannot take the queen.
25...♕xd2 26.♕xb7 ♘d5 27.h6 c3 28.h7 ♕h6 29.♕a7+ ♔c4 30.♗g4
Due to the match situation, White had no other option than to play for a win, but this bishop move isn't really justified. With 30.♕a2+ he could have forced a draw through perpetual check.

This was one of the most spectacular games in the entire World Cup!

30...c2 31.♕a2+

31...♔b4 Black is apparently happy to settle for a draw; otherwise he would have gone for 31...♔d3. After 32.♕a3+ he has 32...♘c3, and the black king is quite safe.
32.♕b2+ ♔c4 33.♖e1

33...♘f4? Strange. Praggnanandhaa had only five minutes left, so you'd think he'd eliminate the white passed pawn with 33...♕xh7. This also yields him control of square e4,

leaving White with empty hands. After 34.♗e2+ ♔c5 35.♕a3+ ♔b6 all hope is lost.
34.h8♕ Certainly not 34.♖e4 ♘fe2+. But White first distracts the black queen, before taking his rook to e4.
34...♕xh8 35.♖e4

Winning one of the knights, and the game.
35...c5 36.♖xf4 ♕xe5 37.♕xc2+ ♔d5 38.♕d2 c4 39.♖xd4+ ♕xd4 40.♗e6+ ♔c5 41.♕xd4+ ♔xd4 42.g4 ♔e5 43.♗f7 ♔f4 44.f3
Black resigned.

This was one of the most spectacular games in the entire World Cup! The young Indian made no mistakes in the tie-breaks. But after that his journey ended. In the next round he was eliminated by an optimally concentrated Maxime Vachier-Lagrave – which is certainly nothing to be ashamed of. ∎

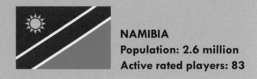
They are The Champions

Ehe 2021 Namibian Championship, held in early May at the Windhoek Country Club Resort, ended in a victory for the highest rated player in the country, 18-year-old IM Dante Beukes. It was his third title, the first time he was only 14 years old. Beukes finished with a perfect score of 9 out of 9, but his win was not a complete walkover. In Round 7, his opponent, Ivan Boois, lost a better position by forfeit when his phone rang. Not in his pocket but in the custody of the arbiter to whom he had handed it before he sat down to play!

Dante started playing at the age of seven, when he joined the chess club at his school. In his debut on the school's chess team he scored zero out of seven, but Dante did not give up and proved himself to be a quick learner. Since then, he has participated in four junior world championships and has represented his country at two Chess Olympiads. He was awarded the title of International Master in 2020 after winning the 2019 African Under-18 championship.

His father has been an essential factor in Dante's chess development, as he accompanied him to international events, taking care of all matters besides chess. Dante has decided to become a full-time chess professional. He works with a coach online on all aspects of the game, with a specific focus on dynamics and calculation. He also writes regularly for *Africa Chess Media*, most recently covering the African players at the 2021 World Cup.

Dante realizes that to become a GM he will have to go abroad. In August he received a chess scholarship from the University of Texas Rio Grande Valley, following in the footsteps of Zambian GM Amon Simutowe, who studied at the University of Dallas and became

DANTE BEUKES
Namibia

the first GM from sub-Saharan Africa.

The following beautiful game, involving three piece sacrifices, Dante played online this year.

Dante Beukes (2206)
Harold Wanyama (2312)
African Online Tornelo Rapid 2021

position after 12...g5

White has played the poisonous 5.c3 in the Sicilian Rossolimo (See Krykun's article in New In Chess Yearbook 135). White sacrifices a pawn to hinder Black's development. Magnus Carlsen has shown how to untangle for Black: ...a6/...b5/...♗b7/...♘c8. Here Black has played ...h6/...g5, weakening his king position. **13.♖c1!** On its way to c5 and possibly f5. **13...a6 14.♗c4 b5 15.♗xf7+** The **first piece sac**, to open up the way to the king. **15...♔xf7 16.♕b3+ ♔f8 17.♖c5 ♘f6** Now 18.♖f5 won't work in view of 18...♗g7. **18.e5 ♗h8**

19.♘xg5 The **second piece sac**. White is threatening mate on f7, so Black has to take. **19...hxg5 20.♘e4 ♔g7 21.♘xg5 ♖f8 22.♕g3 ♔h6 23.e6 dxe6 24.♖xc6 ♕e8** 24...♘xc6 25.♘f7+ ♖xf7 26.♕g6 mate. **25.♘xe6** The **third piece sac**, clearing the g-file for the queen! **25...♗xe6 26.♗xe7 ♕f7 27.♖e1 ♔h7 28.♖exe6 ♗g7 29.h6 ♗e5 30.♕xe5 ♕xf2+ 31.♔h2 ♖f5 32.♕g7** Mate.

Dante is fascinated by the complexity and richness of chess. He says that through his chess journey, he has acquired many qualities that help him in life in general, including accountability, discipline, analytical thinking, perseverance and humility. ∎

*In **They are The Champions** we pay tribute to national champions across the globe. For suggestions please write to editors@newinchess.com.*

Kamil Miton

CURRENT ELO: 2579

DATE OF BIRTH: April 12, 1984

PLACE OF BIRTH: Krakow, Poland

PLACE OF RESIDENCE: Niepolomice, Poland

What is your favourite city?
Krakow.

What was the last great meal you had?
I like going to restaurants with Polish cuisine with friends from my old school.

What drink brings a smile to your face?
Beer.

Which book would you give to a friend?
The *Meditations* of Marcus Aurelius.

Which book are you currently reading?
Many, because I start reading several books at the same time and have problems finishing them.

What is your all-time favourite movie?
Wielki Szu, an old Polish classic about a tricky card player. I've often watched the best moments together with JKD [Jan Krzysztof Duda – ed.].

And your favourite TV series?
Swiat wedlug Kiepskich, a sitcom showing the Polish mentality in a funny way.

Do you have a favourite actor?
Leonardo DiCaprio.

And a favourite actress?
My aunt Ewa Miton, an actress at the well-known Krakow Theater Bagatela.

Is there a work of art that moves you?
I follow Polish painters that fought for independence. Many have tragic biographies. Ludomir Benedyktowicz lost his hands during the uprising of 1863. Thanks to his strong will he created a prosthesis and joined the Munich Academy. He was also a chess player. I am very happy that I have a small painting of his.

What is your earliest chess memory?
When I cried because I did not know how to write down chess moves.

Who is your favourite chess player?
Mikhail Botvinnik. Thanks to him I better understood chess strategy.

Is there a chess book that had a profound influence on you?
The 3 volumes of *Botvinnik's Best Games*.

What was your best result ever?
Silver-medallist at the U20 World Junior Championship when I was 16.

And the best game you played?
Miton-Benjamin, World Open 2005. Five queens happens very rarely ☺.

What was the most exciting chess game you ever saw?
Many classics. Let's say Botvinnik-Capablanca, AVRO 1938, 1-0.

What is your favourite square?
Maybe h1.

Do chess players have typical shortcomings?
They sometimes have problems with simple life duties such as paying bills.

What are chess players particularly good at (except for chess)?
They are smart and original, and they can adapt to many different situations.

Do you have any superstitions concerning chess?
When JKD plays well, we try to do things the same. At the World Cup in Sochi I didn't shave for the whole tournament. Another time we ate kebab every day ☺.

Facebook, Instagram, Snapchat, or?
Instagram, if only for the pictures ☺.

How many Facebook friends do you have? Probably too many.

Who do you follow on Twitter?
I don't use Twitter.

What is your life motto?
Health is the most important thing.

When were you happiest?
When my children were born.

When was the last time you cried?
When cancer defeated my father.

Which three people would you like to invite for dinner?
Thaddeus Kosciusko, Naomi Osaka, John Paul II.

What would people be surprised to know about you?
That my heart is on the right side.

What is your greatest fear?
I hate travelling by plane.

How do you relax?
I spend time with my family and do many sports activities with my sons.

What does it mean to be a chess player?
To be an artist and have freedom.

If you could change one thing in the chess world, what would it be?
Get rid of engines.

What was the best thing that was ever said about chess?
'Talent is the signal to work.'